Joseph Masters

An outline of the Catholic truth

With meditations thereon

Joseph Masters

An outline of the Catholic truth
With meditations thereon

ISBN/EAN: 9783742865083

Manufactured in Europe, USA, Canada, Australia, Japa

Cover: Foto ©Lupo / pixelio.de

Manufactured and distributed by brebook publishing software (www.brebook.com)

Joseph Masters

An outline of the Catholic truth

AN OUTLINE

OF THE

CATHOLIC TRUTH.

WITH

MEDITATIONS THEREON.

LONDON:
JOSEPH MASTERS, 78, NEW BOND STREET.
MDCCCLXXIII.

✢
AD TE DOMINE.

Holy and Undivided Trinity,
One God,
I adore Thee, I worship Thee,
I bless Thee.
Thou hast given me being; I give Thee back Thine own,
O Father Almighty.
Thou hast given me Intellect, Memory, Free-will:
I humbly lay them at Thy feet,
O Jesus, God Incarnate.
Thou hast given me Faith; and by Thy Gift alone can
I confess the Truth,
O Holy Spirit of God.

✢

O Jesus, God Incarnate,
Who didst at the prayer of Thy Ever-Virgin Mother
turn the water into wine, vouchsafe for her sake,
even now,
to strengthen in the Faith, some fainting Heart,
by this draught of water, drawn,
by the hands of the meanest of Thy servants,
from the deep well of
Catholic Truth.

✢

To God, the Three in One, the One in Three,
be glory from all creatures in Heaven, and Earth, and
under the Earth,
through all Eternity.
Amen.

✢

DE SANCTA CRUCE.

Extorquet hoc sorte Dei veniabile signum,
Rusticolas laudes viventi reddere flatu,
In me, qui regit ire lutum plasmabile, Numen
Portio viventum, curatio, fausta medellæ,
Exclusor culpæ, Trinitas effusa, creator:
Cujus honor, lumen, jus, gloria, regna coæve.
Ex fidei merito magnum, pie, reddis Abraham:
Sic Pater, et Genitus, sic Scs Spiritus unus.

Verses at the side.

Eripe credentes, fidei decus, arma salutis:
Munere, Criste, tuo removetur causa reatus.

Verses which form the cross in the middle.

Dulce mihi lignum, pie, majus odore rosetis,
Dumosi colles, lignum, generastis honoris,
Ditans templa Dei crux, et velamen adorans.

NOTE.—This curious acrostic, the production of Venantius H. C. Fortunatus, the friend of Gregory of Tours, and the panegyrist of S. Martin, is given by the Transcriber, in the hope that some more able pen may give an English rendering of this Latin verse of the Sixth Century. The unlearned, but loving heart, will discover in the mystic Triangle and the holy Cross, the hidden teaching of the Creed, the Arms of Salvation and the blessed Wood whereby Righteousness cometh.

AUTHOR'S PREFACE.

IF there be anything contrary to the doctrine of Holy Church in this little work, the error belongs to me, its author, and I hereby submit myself to Her teaching, correction, and judgment.

Passion Week, 1873.

PREFACE.

ALTHOUGH, in the present day, there is no lack of books, both great and small, learned and simple, which treat of the Catholic Faith controversially, and in a dogmatic manner, (and the incalculable good done by such works, GOD alone knows,) yet there still seemed to me room for a book which should set forth the great truths of Religion in systematic sequence, but at the same time viewed rather in their devotional than in their controversial aspect; the present work is an attempt to supply this presumed *desideratum*. It is hoped that it may prove useful to two classes of persons,—to instructed Catholics, who may be pleased to have such an aid in contemplating the great truths which are so dear to them, not as things to be proved, but as Sacred Mysteries to be adduced, who may condescend to use this work as a Guide to the Cathedral of the Faith, which without wearying them with antiquarian details of its architecture, will lead them on from Porch to Nave, from Nave to Quire, from the

Quire to the very Altar, from the Altar to the Chapels of the Saints, and to the Tombs of the Faithful Dead, discoursing only on some of the profound lessons and awful memories which crowd around every stone of the hallowed pile. And it is hoped that it may also prove of use to a certain class of inquirers, *i.e.*, to those whose tender reverent spirits are only repelled and disheartened at the clash of controversial weapons, but who may be led to admire, love, and adore the Truth, when she comes before them, not clad in her warlike armour of controversy, but bearing the gentle emblems of peace.

If any think that an apology is needed for the insertion of texts from the Apocrypha among the passages from Holy Scripture, they may be reminded that the Anglican Church herself quotes the books in question as "Holy Scripture," and as the voice of the HOLY GHOST; neither are the texts given quoted to *prove* any doctrine, but only to illustrate and to throw additional light thereon.

The Editor would ask all who make any use of this book to include both the Author and himself in their intercessions, especially at the Holy Altar.

CONTENTS.

I. THE BEING OF A GOD.

		PAGE
1.	*There is a God*	1
2.	*The Existence of God known both by Nature and Faith*	3
3.	*The Unity of God*	3

II. THE BLESSED TRINITY.

1.	*The Mystery of the Blessed Trinity*	7
2.	*The Trinity*	8
3.	*The Three Divine Persons*	8
4.	*The Father*	8
5.	*The Son*	8
6.	*The Holy Ghost*	9
7.	*The Godhead Equal*	9
8.	*The Operations of the Godhead*	10

III. THE VISIBLE CREATION.

1.	*Creation the work of the Trinity*	16
2.	*Man recognises the Creator in Creation* . . .	17
3.	*God the Creator of all things*	17
4.	*Creation the Act of the Divine Will*	17
5.	*Why diversity in Creation*	18
6.	*God created Heaven and Earth*	18

IV. MAN.

		PAGE
1.	Condition of Man when created	25
2.	Man's Free-will	25
3.	Man's Fall	25

V. THE INCARNATION.

1.	Effect of the Fall	32
2.	Man's Inability to make Reparation	33
3.	God-Incarnate	33
4.	God-Man, the Perfect Mediator	33
5.	Man taken up with God into Heaven	34

VI. THE CATHOLIC CHURCH.

1.	The work of the Incarnation carried on by the Church	42
2.	The Instrumentality by which God the Holy Ghost carries on the work of the Incarnation	43
3.	The Sacraments the Extension of the Incarnation	43
4.	Sacraments the Channels of Divine Grace	44
5.	Baptism	44
6.	Confirmation	44
7.	The Blessed Eucharist	44
8.	Penance	44
9.	Unction of the Sick	44
10.	Holy Orders	45
11.	Marriage	45
12.	The Perpetuity of Divine Grace	45

VII. THE DEPARTED.

1.	Supernatural Life	58
2.	State fixed by Death	58
3.	Growth and Decay of the Soul	58
4.	The Soul conscious of things of earth	59
5.	Prayers of the Faithful Departed	60
6.	Efficacy of Prayers of and for the Departed	60
7.	Prayers of the Lost unheard	60

VIII. THE JUDGMENT.

		PAGE
1.	*The World purified by Fire*	67
2.	*The Advent*	68
3.	*The Judge*	68
4.	*The Witnesses*	68
5.	*The Scrutiny*	68

IX. THE FINAL DECISION.

1.	*The Sentence Irreversible*	76
2.	*The Separation Eternal*	76
3.	*Condemnation Eternal*	76
4.	*Bliss Eternal*	76

APPENDIX.

Texts of Holy Scripture . . . 81

The letters affixed to the references given in the 'Texts' refer to the Scriptural passages given in full in the Appendix.

AN OUTLINE OF THE CATHOLIC TRUTH.

GOD.

The Prayer.

GOD, Essence beyond Essence, Nature Increate, GOD Eternal, I prostrate myself before Thee, and I worship Thee with the full devotion of soul, and mind, and body. O my GOD, Thou alone knowest the unworthiness of this Thy servant. Bear with me whilst I dare to meditate of Thee. Guide me whilst I ponder, for not in presumption, O LORD, not in presumption, but in humility and faith, do I now venture to think of Thee, O GOD my GOD.

I. THE BEING OF A GOD.

The Texts.

1. The Catholic Faith holds that there is a GOD, that GOD is. Catholic doctrine teaches that GOD is Self-Exist-

   1. *There is a God.*

ent—the First Cause; Essential Essence. "Infinite SPIRIT in the state of Personality;" without Beginning, without End; the Supreme Good. Incomprehensible,—since none but GOD can comprehend GOD. Apprehensible,—so far as He chooses to reveal Himself to the Supernatural Capacity which He has Himself created within man to receive the knowledge of His Being. Filling all things, yet restricted by none. Knowing all things, yet fully known by none. Ever-existing;—there never was a time when He was not. Ever-abiding;—there never will be a time when He ceases to be. All things depend on Him; all things were made by Him, yet dependeth He on none. (Bear with me, O my GOD, while I try to stammer of Thy Greatness.) GOD is that He is, GOD Almighty. But except He had revealed Himself to His Church, who had dared to speak of Him, for who hath by searching found out GOD? Behold, I go forward, but He is not there; and backward, but I cannot perceive Him: on the left hand where He doth work, but I cannot behold Him: He hideth Himself on the right hand, that I cannot see Him: but He knoweth the way that I take.

Job 11. 7.
Job 23. 8-10.

There is a GOD. GOD is. GOD is a pure, incomprehensible Spirit, Incorporeal, Self-Existent. GOD is Unutterable, Infinite. GOD is

ᵃ S. Jo. 4. 24.
ᵇ Job 11. 7-9.
ᶜ Jud. 13. 18.
ᵈ Is. 40. 25, 28.

Being. The Origin, the Alpha; the Omega, the Final End.

^a Rev. 1. 8.

2. He that cometh to GOD must believe that He is. The existence of GOD is not, strictly speaking, of Faith, since it is evident to natural reason. The natural light of Reason suffices to prove it. Our knowledge of the existence of creatures, necessarily obliges us to know that there is a Creator. But to those who are unlearned, or who are not endowed with great reasoning powers, the knowledge of the existence of GOD often comes by the way of Faith, for GOD has also revealed this Truth, and the Church commands it to be received.

2. The Existence of God known both by Nature and Faith.

^a Heb. 11. 6.
^b Rom. 1. 19, 20.
^c Wisd. 13. 1, 4, 5.
^d Acts 14. 17.

3. GOD is the Supreme GOD, therefore GOD is One. GOD is Eternal, Infinite in existence; there never was a time when He is not. GOD is a SPIRIT. He is the First Cause. He created all things out of nothing. GOD is Simple Essence; One, Indivisible. GOD is perfect; infinite in Perfection; Unchangeable. GOD is Essential Wisdom, Essential Love. GOD is His own Essence. GOD is GOD. I Am That I Am.

3. The Unity of God.

^a Isa. 45. 5.
^b S. Jo. 4. 24.
^c Job 38. 4-6.
^d Deut. 6. 4.
^e S. Mat. 5. 48.
^f Isa. 40. 28.
^g 1 S. Jo. 4. 16.
^h Exod. 3. 14.

The Meditation.

GOD makes Himself known to man by the light of Reason with

God Revealed to Man's Reason.

which He has endowed him, and He reflects Himself in the mirror of His creation. That which may be known of GOD is manifest to them; for GOD hath showed it unto them. For the invisible things of Him from the creation of the world are clearly seen, being understood by the things that are made, even His Eternal Power and Godhead.

<small>Ro. 1. 19, 20.</small>

Man cannot but believe in the existence of a GOD; his own existence convinces him; "it is needless to prove to a son the existence of his father." His own reason has bidden him fall down and worship the Infinite, the Unknown, the Illimitable, even though the jar of the Fall have warped his reason and distorted his vision, so that he vainly tries to grasp the Supernatural by the natural, and to confine the Infinite in space; or to frame his stammering tongue to speak the unutterable words, and to name the Unknown Name of the Unknown GOD. GOD had not indeed left Himself without a witness which man's reason grasped, in common too, it may be, with the whole creation, for all things serve Him. The lions roaring after their prey, do seek their meat from GOD. The eyes of all wait upon Him, and He giveth them their meat in due season. He openeth His Hand, and filleth all things living with plenteousness. All His works praise Him, and own Him LORD.

<small>Ps. 104. 21.</small>

<small>Ps. 145. 15, 16.</small>

<small>Job 38. 11.</small>

The proud waves of the sea are stayed before Him, and they know the glorious voice of the LORD; the earth trembleth at the look of Him; Ps. 29. 4. if He do but touch the hills they smoke. Ps. 104. 32.

But not in the Book of His Vi- *God known by* sible Creation which man's reason *Revelation.* suffices him to read, did GOD alone reveal Himself. It pleased Him to place the supernatural lamp of Revelation in the safe keeping of His Church, and to implant within the soul of man 1 Cor. 2. 4, 5, the supernatural eye of faith, whereby he could 10. apprehend this Divine Light, and he who by searching could not find out GOD, stands trembling at the foot of Sinai, while GOD proclaims Himself the Great I AM. I, the LORD, and none else; there is no GOD beside Me. I girded thee, though Thou hast not known Me. I am Isa. 45. 5, 6, the LORD, and there is none else. I form the 7, 22. light, and create darkness. I am GOD, and there is none else.

In the thick trees of Paradise, in the flood of Gen. 3. 8. Gen. 7. 15, 16. raging waters, in deep sleep, and in the horror Gen. 15. 1-17. of great darkness, in the burning bush, and in Ex. 19. 16-19. the fires of Sinai, in the rifts of the half-opened Ezek. 1. 4. Isa. 6. 1, 2. heavens, in the lions' den, and in the furnace Dan. 6. 22. Dan. 3. 25. of Babylon, by Adam, Noah, Abram, Moses, Isaiah, Ezekiel, Daniel, the Three Faithful Children, the Voice of the Almighty GOD is heard; above the water-flood, above the storm, above the raging of the flames, GOD, Almighty, Infinite, Eternal. And the Catholic Church echoes the Divine word, and proclaims the faith in GOD. Not by the wisdom of the world, not by man's teaching, not by the light of fallible reason, but by supernatural, infallible Revelation she affirms everywhere, always, and for ever, her belief in GOD.

Yet again, by reason also man has conceived the Infinite. He has conceived the Being of a GOD. His reason has touched the limit beyond which it cannot go; it has met the Supernatural. Jacob has wrestled until the break of day, and has seen GOD Face to face. He halts upon his thigh, for the angel of GOD has touched the sinew of his reason, and it shrinks. Henceforth it must stand aside, and suffer him to be led by faith, but he has prevailed, and his name shall be called no more Jacob, but Israel, for he has seen GOD Face to face. He has acknowledged the First Truth, the Being of a GOD. By the highest exercise of the strongest reason, he has reached the dawn of Faith. "The day breaketh." He believes in GOD, and passes on into the full light of the perfect day to the doctrine of the Blessed TRINITY.

THE BLESSED TRINITY.

The Prayer.

HOLY, Holy, Holy, LORD GOD Almighty, before Thee angels and archangels bow; before Thee the six-winged seraphim do veil their faces; before Thee the whole earth keeps still silence, and how shall my unclean heart meditate of the Majesty of the Trinal Unity? how think of the Mystery of the Unity in TRINITY? Touch Thou my lips and heart, O LORD, with the Live Coal from off Thine Altar, and then shall the string of my tongue be loosed, and I be enabled to speak plain, and to utter Thy Truth.

II. THE BLESSED TRINITY.

The Texts.

1. The Catholic Faith holds that this GOD, Essential in Unity, is Three in Person; One GOD in Trinity, and Trinity in Unity. Catholic doctrine teaches that the Unity in Trinity, and the Trinity in Unity is to be worshipped: that the Godhead of the FATHER, of the SON, and of the HOLY GHOST, is all One: the Glory Equal, the Majesty Co-Eternal.

1. The Mystery of the Blessed Trinity.

It is granted that GOD is, and that GOD is One. It is the Omega of Reason, the Alpha of Faith. *The knowledge of God, what it is.*

2. The Nature of that GOD, the Doctrine of the Trinity is the next link in the eternal chain of Truth. GOD One in Essence is Three in Person. *2. The Trinity.*

ᵃ Rev. 4. 8.
ᵇ Rev. 1. 8.

3. The Three Divine Persons are revealed to man as FATHER, SON, and HOLY GHOST. The FATHER begets the SON ; the HOLY GHOST proceeds from the FATHER and the SON ; and the Three Persons are Co-Eternal and Co-Equal.[1] *3. The Three Divine Persons.*

ᵃ S. Mat. 28. 19.
ᵇ Ps. 2. 7.
ᶜ S. Mat. 3. 16, 17.
ᵈ S. Jo. 1. 18.
ᵉ S. Jo. 16. 13, 14.
ᶠ S. Jo. 14, 26.
ᵍ S. Jo. 15. 26.
ʰ Rom. 8. 9.
ⁱ Gal. 4. 6.
ʲ 1 S. Jo. 5. 7.

4. The FATHER is the Fountain whence the other two Sacred Persons proceed ; yet He was not before them, for they came forth from Him, and yet continued with Him, from everlasting before time was ; He never was without them ; He is not greater in nature than they are, since they are of the same substance with Himself; His SON proceeds from Himself alone after an unspeakable manner, which revelation declares to be best named to us as " generation ;" His SPIRIT proceeds from Himself, (and, as His SON shares all things with Him, from His SON likewise,) the Procession of the SPIRIT is revealed to us under no other name. *4. The Father.*

ᵃ S. Jo. 8. 42.
ᵇ S. Jo. 15. 26.
ᶜ S. Jo. 1. 1, 2.
ᵈ 1 Cor. 2. 9-11.
ᵉ Eph. 2. 18.
ᶠ 1 S. Jo. 5. 7.
ᵍ Heb. 1. 5, 8.
ʰ S. Jo. 5. 23.
ⁱ S. Jo. 8. 19, 42.
ʲ S. Jo. 10. 30.
ᵏ S. Jo. 14. 26.
ˡ S. Jo. 15. 26.
ᵐ S. Jo. 7. 39.

5. "GOD, when He begat the *5. The Son.*

---
[1] See Creed of S. Athanasius.

WORD, begat that which is Himself." Him Who is the Wisdom of GOD, existing from all eternity, Co-Eternal with GOD; there never was a time when that Wisdom was not with GOD, and when that Wisdom was not GOD. The SON is of the Substance of the FATHER, the Sole-Begotten.

^a Col. ii. 9.
^b Col. i. 17.
^c Isa. 9. 6.
^d S. Jo. 14. 9, 11.

6. The HOLY GHOST is GOD; a Divine Person, Co-Equal, and Co-Eternal with the Divine Person of the FATHER, and with the Divine Person of the SON. He is the Love of GOD, existing from all eternity, Co-Eternal with GOD; there never was a time when that Love was not with GOD, and when that Love was not GOD.

6. The Holy Ghost.

^a 1 Cor. 2. 10, 11.
^b Eph. 2. 18.
^c Eph. 4. 4.
^d 1 S. Jo. 4. 16.
^e 2 Cor. 3. 17.

7. The Godhead of the FATHER, of the SON, and of the HOLY GHOST is all One. In all things the Unity in Trinity, and the Trinity in Unity is to be worshipped. The FATHER, the SON, and the HOLY GHOST are One in Substance, and of inseparable Equality; One GOD, Unity in Essence, and Plurality in Person. Yet they are not Three GODS, but One GOD. The FATHER is not the SON nor the HOLY GHOST; the SON is not the FATHER nor the HOLY GHOST; the HOLY GHOST is not the FATHER nor the SON. But the HOLY GHOST is GOD; the FATHER is GOD; the SON is GOD; and these Three are One.

7. The Godhead Equal.

^a 2 Cor. 13. 14.
^b S. Mat. 28. 19.
^c Rev. 4. 17.

8. No operation of the FATHER is without the SON and the HOLY GHOST: no operation of the SON is without the FATHER and the HOLY GHOST; no operation of the HOLY GHOST is without the FATHER and the SON; for these Three are One.

^a S. Jo. 5. 19.
^b S. Jo. 5. 20.
^c S. Jo. 10. 32, 37, 38.
^d S. Jo. 16. 13.
^e 1 Cor. 12. 3-6.

8. The Operations of the Godhead.

The Meditation.

Lift up thyself, my soul, far above all earthly thoughts and imaginations. Put the sandals of carnal understanding from off thy feet, for thou art standing on the threshold of heaven. Bow down thyself, my soul, bow down thyself into the profound abyss of thine own nothingness, for thy GOD reveals Himself to thee. The awful chords of the Trisagion, the Heaven-inspired song: "Holy GOD, Holy Mighty, Holy Immortal," are ringing through the highest Heaven, and thine ear perchance may catch the faint echoes of the melodies of Paradise.

It was the special office of the Catholic Church to unfold the doctrine of the Blessed Trinity to man, yet GOD left not Himself without a witness, for man himself in his threefold nature of spirit, soul, and body, shadows forth the ever-indestructible Likeness and Image of GOD in which he was created. The spirit pervading every part of the whole body, yet restricted to no part,—

Man, a witness in himself to the truth of the Trinity.

invisible, immortal, intangible. The sentient soul thinking, seeing, hearing, speaking, itself unseen, yet apparent. The body visible, tangible, mortal, yet its mortality imbued with immortality. The threefold being one. The one in three. Man himself in his own mysterious being shadowed forth the Ever-Blessed Trinity.

Nature's voice was not silent. The ever flowing water, the solid ice, the uprising dew, day by day, morning by morning, proclaimed the Tri-Une GOD; but it spoke in mystic language, for man's carnal nature had waxed gross, and his supernatural faculties were clouded, and he saw but faintly through the thick darkness, yet this Truth was secretly brought to him, and his ear received a little thereof, but it came to him as in thoughts from the visions of the night, for deep sleep had fallen upon him. Yet the GOD-implanted truth struggled for expression, and in the dark stone caves of Elephanta, the teaching of the metaphysical Brahmin embodied itself, and left its record standing through long centuries, a lasting monument of the inadequacy of intellect to reach the Supernatural, which is above it. They groped for the wall like the blind, and they groped as if they had no eyes; they stumbled at noonday as in the night. They had caught a faint reflex glimpse of the Eternal Light of

The Witness of Nature.

Job 4. 12, 13.

Isa. 59. 10.

Truth, and its dazzling beauty blinded and intoxicated them. Professing themselves to be wise, they became fools, and changed the glory of the Uncorruptible GOD into an image made like to corruptible man.

<small>Ro. 1. 22, 23.</small>

Even the Jewish Church but guessed at this eternal truth. Yet GOD had vouchsafed by type and figure, and even in express words to declare Himself. On the very threshold of Revelation, GOD said, Let us make man in our image, after our likeness. To the Father of the faithful the LORD appeared. Abraham sat in the tent door, in the heat of the day, (to mortal man shone forth the noonday brightness of Divine Truth,) and he lift up his eyes, and looked, and lo, three men stood by him. Moses sang of the Trinity in Unity in his first song of triumph. The Jewish Priest opened not his lips to bless but in the Name of the Tri-Une GOD. The mystic Three in One in type and action runs through the whole of the Blessed Written Word of GOD, and repeats itself like the rhythm of the language of Heaven. In the oft repeated declaration: I, the LORD, your GOD; and in the unwilling utterance of Balaam, we hear the same Truth. Again in the thrice repeated call to Samuel, ere the lamp of GOD went out in the Temple of the LORD; and notwithstanding the

<small>*The Witness of the Old Testament.*</small>

<small>Gen. 1. 26.</small>
<small>Gen. 18. 1, 2.</small>

<small>Ex. 15. 16-18.</small>
<small>Nu. 6. 24-26.</small>

<small>Ex. 8. 27.</small>
<small>Ex. 10. 22.</small>
<small>Num. 10. 33.</small>

<small>Lev. 23. 43, &c.</small>
<small>Num. 24. 16, 17.</small>

<small>1 Sam. 3. 1-9.</small>

eyes of men, like those of Eli, began to wax dim, and they could not see, and the Glorious Truth was veiled, yet could it not be wholly hidden, until with a flood of heavenly brightness it burst forth, and to Isaiah it was given to be- Isa. 6. 1-4. hold the vision of the LORD and His Glory, and to hear the mystic strains of the Ter-Sanctus, Holy, Holy, Holy, the LORD of Hosts. Again, shrouded in more dazzling glory of light ineffable unto which no man may approach, did the Tri-Une GOD reveal Himself to Ezekiel by the Ezek. 1. 26-28. river Chebar. To the chaste Daniel, it was Dan. 7. 9. granted to behold the Eternal SON, the Ancient of Days; and the sound of the Seven-fold SPIRIT Isa. 11. 2. Joel 2. 28. of GOD became clearer as the dawn approached.

The Jewish Church also had her Office Book, the Psalter of David, wherein the sweet Psalmist sang to the Blessed GOD, and glorified the FATHER, the GOD of all Gods; the SON, the LORD; the HOLY SPIRIT, the LORD of all Ps. 136. 1-3. Lords. He drew aside the veil from the highest Sanctuary, and in the wonderful 110th Psalm uttered the mystic Dialogue of the TRINITY. Ps. 110. Scarcely a Psalm but speaks of the Unity in Trinity, of the Trinity in Unity. But it remained for the Bride, the Catholic Church, to reveal to man, the LORD GOD Almighty, as she had learned it from the lips of her *The Church reveals the Mystery of the Blessed Trinity.*

LORD Himself. And in the short formula which she teaches her children to repeat after each Psalm: Glory be to the FATHER, and to the SON, and to the HOLY GHOST; As it was in the beginning, is now, and ever shall be, world without end. Amen: is embodied the sum of Catholic Truth.

<small>S. Mat. 28. 19.</small>

O my GOD, One, Eternal, Uncreated, Incomprehensible, I worship Thee, FATHER, SON, and HOLY GHOST, Unity in Trinity, Trinity in Unity, GOD, Blessed for ever, I worship Thee.

The Church drawing deep from the ever-springing well of Holy Scripture, the perennial fountain of Divine Truth, teaches her children to adore GOD the FATHER, the Creator of all things; GOD the SON, the Word; and GOD the HOLY GHOST, the LORD, the Giver of Life.

<small>*Three Divine Persons in One Godhead.*</small>

<small>Gen. 1. 1.
Isa. 42. 5.
S. John 1. 1.
S. Jo. 14. 17.
S. Jo. 15. 26.
S. Jo. 16. 15.
1 S. Jo. 5. 7.</small>

GOD'S Truth is One. Nature had spoken the same language, and in the created relationship of father and son, GOD faintly shadowed forth to man the Incarnate Mystery of the Eternal FATHER and the Eternal SON. The FATHER Who begets, the SON Who is begotten. Very GOD of Very GOD. But in natural relationship there exists no type of the HOLY SPIRIT. Aweful in His Being, aweful in His Essence, the Church bows down before His eternal Godhead, and confesses that the HOLY GHOST is

GOD. And again, in this Trinity none is afore or after other; none is greater, or less than another; but the whole Three Persons are Co-Eternal together, and Co-equal.

Mystery of Mysteries, how shall frail man grasp Thee? Reason cannot contain that which is above itself. GOD in that He is GOD cannot be understood by man. Were He comprehended or comprehensible by man He were not GOD. But man was created in the likeness of GOD, endowed with supernatural faculties wherewith he may attain by faith to the knowledge of the Most High. O Faith, great gift of GOD, worthy of the Divine Giver, by thee I acknowledge and confess the Belief which the Catholic Church teaches and hath taught always, everywhere and for ever, the Faith of the Blessed TRINITY. *The Mystery apprehended by Faith.*

GOD, the Three in One, the One in Three, has revealed Himself in His Church by the three-fold teaching of His Visible Creation, His Written Word, and His Incarnate Word. The third successive link in the golden chain of Faith which binds earth to Heaven, and which discloses the relations of GOD to man, and of man to GOD, is then The Visible Creation.

THE VISIBLE CREATION.

The Prayer.

O LORD GOD Almighty, Creator of Heaven and earth, I worship Thee. The soul which Thou hast created thirsteth for Thee; the flesh which Thou hast made longeth after Thee. Open Thou mine eyes, O FATHER, that I may see Thee in the Heavens the work of Thine hands; strengthen Thou my sight, O Sole-Begotten, that I may behold Thee in the sea whose waves grew calm beneath Thy sacred feet. Waken mine ears, O HOLY SPIRIT, that I may hear Thy voice among the trees of the wood, as Thou fliest upon the wings of the wind. Set my heart at liberty that I may praise Thee with all Thy creatures upon earth.

O LORD my GOD and FATHER, put clay upon mine eyes that I may see. Say unto me, Ephphatha, that I may hear. Touch Thou my tongue that I may speak plain, and tell of all Thy wondrous works.

III. THE VISIBLE CREATION.

The Texts.

1. The Catholic Faith holds that GOD the Blessed TRINITY created *1. Creation the work of the Trinity.*

Heaven and earth and all that therein is. Catholic doctrine teaches that Creation was called into being by the Will of GOD, and that it unfolds to us the Paternity of GOD, the Power of GOD, and the Love of GOD. It teaches us to worship "GOD the FATHER Almighty, Maker of Heaven and earth; GOD the SON, by Whom all things were made," and "GOD the HOLY GHOST, the LORD and Giver of Life."

In the beginning GOD created the heavens and the earth. He created; that is, out of nothing He caused that to be which had no being. He is the Creator. The power to create pertains to GOD alone. Creation is the work of the TRINITY. ^a Gen. 1. 1. ^b Gen. 1-3. ^c S. Jo. 1. 3. ^d Ephes. 3. 9. ^e Ps. 104. 30.

2. Man knows GOD as the Creator by that part of His Creation of which he is cognizant, viz., the earth upon which he dwells, and all that is therein, and the material heavens which are above him. *2. Man recognises the Creator in Creation.* ^a Rom. 1. 20.

3. All things were made by GOD, and without Him was not anything made that was made. GOD is the Universal Cause of all existence, whether angelic and incorporeal, or material and corporeal. *3. God the Creator of all things.* ^a S. Jo. 1. 3. ^b Rom. 11. 36. ^c Isa. 45. 6, 7, 18.

4. The universe was created by a pure act of the Divine Will. The Creator is Eternal; neither intellect nor matter *4. Creation the Act of the Divine Will.* ^a Ps. 33. 6-9.

are eternal. GOD had no need of creation ; He created by a pure act of Divine goodness.

5. In the Creation the finite crea- ture beholds the reflex image of the Infinite Creator, hence, multiplicity, diversity, order, each in its own sphere revealing to man something of the nature of Him Who created ; in GOD all is ONE, but man must learn of Him in parts.

5. Why Diversity in Creation.

ᵃ Job 38-40.

6. GOD created the Heavenly Hierarchy, He also created the material universe, but whether at the same time is not revealed. GOD made the world for man; GOD made man for Himself.

6. God created Heaven and earth.

ᵃ Heb. 1. 7.
ᵇ Dan. 7. 10.
ᶜ Heb. 1. 14.
ᵈ Job 38. 7.
ᵉ Ps. 68. 17.
ᶠ 1 Cor. 3. 21-23.

The Meditation.

In bliss unutterable, perfection incomprehensible, love unfathomable, the Trinal Godhead is, without need, or want, or lack.

O my GOD, be Thou with my mouth, for I am slow of tongue, and dumb, even as it were a beast before Thee, when I search in vain for words to tell of Thy Majesty.

Out of pure infinite goodness, by an act of the Divine Will, GOD created. The fiat of the Almighty called out of nothing, the mighty universe.

In the beginning,—in the remote ages, all but eternal ; in time, yet defying human calculation,

Gen. 1. 1.
2 S. Pet. 3. 5.

GOD created the heaven and the earth, By the word of GOD the heavens were of old, and all the hosts of them were made by the breath of His mouth. Thrones and Dominions, Principalities and Powers, Cherubim and Seraphim, Angels and Archangels, created by the Almighty Word, bowed down before the eternal throne; thousand thousands ministered unto Him Who sat thereon, and ten thousand times ten thousand stood before Him. The song of angelic praise rang through the vaulted roof of the highest Heaven. The noise of their wings was like the noise of great waters, as the Voice of the Almighty, the voice of speech, as the noise of a host. In their midst was the Covering Cherub, Lucifer, son of the morning, the sum of created perfection, full of wisdom, and perfect in beauty. Eden was his, Eden, the Garden of GOD. Every precious stone was his covering; the sardius, topaz, and the diamond, the beryl, the onyx, and the jasper, the sapphire, the emerald, and the carbuncle, and the gold. Sweetly sounded forth the music of his tabrets and his pipes upon the holy mountain of his GOD, as he walked up and down in the midst of the stones of fire. O Covering Cherub, wherefore didst thou turn thy gaze from uncreated beauty to behold thine own! O Lucifer, Son of the Morning, how art thou fallen! Now art

Ps. 33. 6.

Dan. 7. 10.

Ezek. 1.

Ezek. 28.

Isa. 14. 13.
Ezek. 28.

thou as profane cast out of the Mountain of GOD, now are the thrones cast down, and thy place is found no more in Heaven. The voice of thy praise is hushed, thy beauty is withered, thy wisdom has been corrupted and thou art brought down to the pit. Darkness is upon the face of the deep, and thine Eden, blasted by the sirocco of thy pride, is without form and void.

<small>Dan. 4. 31. Rev. 12.</small>

All was wrapped in the blackness of darkness. GOD'S wrath had declared itself; His justice had vindicated itself, and there are vacant thrones in Heaven. And now the Eternal Spirit of Love, flowing forth ineffably from the Eternal FATHER and the Eternal SON, brooded upon the face of the waters. The Voice of GOD spake the word. He bowed the Heavens and came down. He rode upon the Cherubims and did fly, and at the brightness of His Presence His clouds removed, the foundations of the round world were discovered, for GOD, even the most mighty GOD, had spoken, and there was light. Then the morning stars sang together, and all the sons of GOD shouted for joy, and the first day dawned upon the earth.

<small>Ps. 18.</small>

<small>Job 38. 7.</small>

The second day, while yet the earth was standing out of the water and in the water, the LORD spread out the heavens like a vault; He measured the waters in the hollow of His hand, and meted out heaven with a span, and the

<small>2 S. Pet. 3. 5. 2 Esd. 16. 59. Isa. 40. 12.</small>

firmament was where hitherto there had been illimitable space.

On the third day, the sea brake forth as if it had issued from the womb, and the LORD made the thick clouds the garment thereof, and thick darkness a swaddling band for it, and set its bounds beyond which it could not pass, and made the grains of sand a barrier of its proud waves. He gathered the waters of the sea together as it were upon an heap; and laid up the deep as in a treasure house. The LORD sitteth above the water-flood, and the LORD remaineth a King for ever. O LORD, how glorious are Thy works; an unwise man doth not well consider this, and a fool doth not understand it! *Job 38. Ps. 33. 7. Ps. 29. 9. Ps. 92. 5, 6.*

The morning of that third mystic day dawned also upon the earth, whose foundations He had laid; the mountains were molten under Him, the valleys were cleft as wax before the fire. He stood and measured the earth; He beheld, and drove asunder the nations: and the everlasting mountains were scattered, and the perpetual hills did bow. The mountains saw Him and trembled, the overflowing of the water passed by; the deep uttered his voice, and lifted up his hands on high. Then did all the trees of the wood also rejoice before the LORD, His voice shook the wilderness, yea, the LORD *Mic. 1. 4. Hab. 3. 6. Ps. 96. 12. Ps. 29. 7. Isa. 35. 1, 2.*

shook the wilderness of Cades. The solitary places were glad, and the desert did rejoice and blossom as the rose. It did blossom abundantly, and rejoiced even with joy and singing; the glory of Lebanon was given unto it, the excellency of Carmel and Sharon; for already the Throne of the Incarnate GOD was being prepared upon earth, and GOD, Who reigneth from the Tree, saw that the works of that day were good.

Ps. 8.

O LORD our Governor, how excellent is Thy Name in all the world; Thou that hast set Thy glory above the heavens. Lift up thine eyes, O son of man, and consider the work of the fourth day, the heavens, even the works of His fingers, the moon and the stars which He hath ordained bow down and worship Him. Seek Him that maketh the seven stars and Orion, that bringeth forth the twelve signs in their seasons, that guideth Arcturus with his sons, and turneth the shadow of death into the morning, and maketh the day dark with night: the LORD is His Name. The sun and moon stood still in their habitation: at the light of His arrows they go, and at the shining of His glittering spear. His glory covereth the heavens, and the earth is full of His praise.

Amos 5. 8.
Job 38. 32.

O praise the LORD of Heaven; praise Him in the height. Praise Him, all ye angels of His; praise Him, all His host. Praise Him, thou sun, who wilt hereafter shroud thy brightness in the darkness of Calvary; and thou moon, whose pitying beams will gleam through the olive boughs of Gethsemane. Praise Him, ye stars, which will shine above His manger-bed, and thou light, wherewith He will clothe Himself, as with raiment glistering white as snow on Tabor. Praise Him Who made you, for He beheld you, the work of His hands; He looked upon all the work of that fourth glorious day, and pronounced it good.

The stars rejoiced in their courses, but there was still silence in the mighty waters, still silence in the sun-lit air, and once more the fiat of the Almighty went forth, and the waters brought forth abundantly, and winged fowl flew in the firmament of heaven. GOD blessed them, and the fifth morning had dawned, but silence yet reigned over hill and valley, mountain and wilderness, and again GOD spake, and the green earth brought forth the living creature after its kind, and GOD saw that it was good. From earth, and sea, and sky, ascended the threefold Sanctus to the Thrice Holy GOD; and as yet no discord marred the harmony. Earth's voices floated upwards unopposed and mingled with the song of the Heavenly Host, as they worshipped the LORD GOD Almighty, Which was, and is, and is to come.

Isa. 45. 18. And now the work of Creation did but await its completion. For thus saith the LORD that created the heavens : GOD Himself that formed the earth and made it : He hath established it, He created it not in vain, He formed it to be inhabited, and the world being thus made, replenished, and adorned, there is as it were a pause. The Three Divine Persons take Ineffable Counsel, and the result of that Divine Counsel is the creation of Man.

MAN.

The Prayer.

O Thou Who inspirest the thoughts and cogitations of man's heart, be with me that I may ponder worthily of man the noblest work of Thy creation. O LORD GOD, Who didst form man from the dust of the ground, open my eyes that I may understand somewhat of his twofold mysterious nature, half Divine, half earthy. O Thou Who didst breathe into his nostrils the breath of life, illumine my soul with supernatural vision, that I may discern Thine Image and Likeness, beneath the clay wherein Thou hast concealed It. And bow Thou down my heart before Thy Majesty that I may meditate reverently of him, who, although fallen, yet bears the Impress of Thy Likeness.

IV. MAN.

The Texts.

1. Man was created in the Image and after the Likeness of GOD. He was the completion, the summit of creation, which without him was imperfect. He was composed of soul and body; the soul, created by the inspiration of GOD; the body, made from the dust of the ground which GOD had created. He was destined for immortality, endued with every supernatural grace. He possessed intelligence, will, free-will, memory and reason; and all these in the highest perfection. He was good, holy, pure; able to hold converse with GOD. He had dominion over all the lower creation; he was its head.

1. Condition of man when created.
a Ge. 1. 27, 28.
b Gen. 2. 7.
c Ecclus. 17. 1-3.
d Ecclus. 17. 6-13.
e Gen. 3. 8.
f Ecclus. 17. 4.
g Ps. 8. 5, 6.

2. Man was free, not an automaton; therefore he must needs be put to the proof. He was vulnerable, capable of proof. He was a compound being, and the test touched his spiritual and his material nature.

2. Man's Free-will.
a Ecclus. 15. 14-17.
b Gen. 3. 6.
c 1 Tim. 2. 14.

3. Man fell; he conceived sin in will; he cast himself down. Then the ser-

3. Man's Fall.
a Wis. 2. 23, 24.

pent, himself already irredeemably fallen, had
the advantage over him. The sin conceived in
will was carried out in deed. The indestructible
Likeness of GOD was thereby indeed blurred,
distorted, and defaced, but it did not wholly
perish. Man retained the Divine Impress, for
it was ineffaceable.

b Rom. 6. 16.
c S. Jude 6.
d S. Ja. 4. 7.
e Heb. 1. 11.

The Meditation.

Earth, and sky, and ocean, were spread out
in perfect beauty before the LORD their Creator.
But one spot there was in which was gathered
together all that was fair and beautiful; it was
Eden, the garden of the LORD.

Divine counsel had been held; *Man created in God's Image.* the will of the TRINITY was declared, and GOD created man in His own Image after their likeness; male and female created He them, and He placed them in the Paradise which 'The Gardener' had planted, eastward in Eden. From the dust of the ground He formed him, and breathed into his nostrils the breath of life, and man became a living soul.

Ge. 1. 26, 27.

Gen. 2. 7.

S. Joh. 20. 13.

Perfect in himself, bearing the Divine Image of Him Who was in the fulness of time, according to the eternal counsels of GOD, to humble Himself and take upon Him His servant's form, Adam furnished from his own body the substance from which Eve was builded. Mystic

Gal. 4. 4.
Phil. 2. 5-7.
1 S. Pet. 1. 20.

Gen. 2. 21-24.

type of CHRIST and His Church, foreshadowed from the very beginning of creation ; and no marvel, for this was the very end and purpose of Creation. Man was as it were the canvas on which GOD portrayed the Likeness of His SON ; the rough cast and model of the future perfect work.

Perfect in wisdom, perfect in intelligence, Adam stood before his Maker, the masterpiece of His works, and GOD looked on him, and blessed him. _{Gen. 1.28,31.}

Our fallen nature must needs climb upwards to his perfection ; our sensual nature stands entranced in mute amazement, gazing solely upon the marvellous beauty of his form, the strength of his intellect, the mighty grasp of that intelligence which comprehended all the secrets of GOD's creation, as the creatures He had made passed before their earthly lord and master to do him homage, and to receive from him their name. But the surpassing dignity of man consisted in the supernatural beauty of the soul, bearing the Image of GOD. This was the jewel of priceless worth, placed in a casket most beautiful, it is true, but as frail as beautiful. _{Gen. 2. 19.}

Unrestricted to any part of the body, yet governing every movement of it ; transfusing every particle of it, but not yet cleaving to the dust of which it was made, the soul was at once the shadow of God's Omnipotence ;—spirit, soul, and body, united yet distinct ;—man bore about in his very being the Mystery of the Trinity. Possessing unwavering Faith in the Blessed God, unbounded Hope in the Divine goodness, and fervent Charity for the Love itself from Whose very fount it had been freshly kindled, his soul reflected in its supernatural graces the Likeness of the Blessed Father. With clear, undimmed vision he could look upon the Face of God, —nothing came between that perfect soul and it. Sin had not as yet compelled man to cover his face ; it shone with the reflex beauty of God, but there were not as yet the fallen children of men to fear the presence of Holiness. As yet the body, untainted by corruption, pressed not down the soul ; as yet the earthy tabernacle weighed not down the mind, but Adam held converse with his Maker, and looked upon his Majesty unscathed.

The casket which contained the soul was moulded by the hand of God Himself ; with infinite care the Potter, and the Carpenter, and the Refiner of Silver, had moulded and shaped and adorned with exquisite workmanship the Tabernacle in which hereafter the Blessed Host was to repose. It was faultless, so that the Psalmist considering its beauty even after it had fallen, and the Royal Image that had been so defaced that it was but faintly, although unmistakeably perceptible, exclaimed, "I will give thanks unto Thee, for I am fearfully and wonderfully made ; marvellous are Thy works, and that my soul knoweth right well."

This glorious creature was free. *Man's will* GOD, Whose service is perfect free-*free.* dom, did not withhold from man His own attribute of will ; He moreover left that will free and unfettered. Adam was free to choose the service of the great GOD and sovereign LORD Who had created him out of nothing, and formed him from the dust of the ground,—or, to usurp authority over himself, and to make of himself his own god. GOD is a GOD of liberty, and He wills that they who serve Him should be free. With the very gifts which He had lavished upon man, man could serve Him or rebel against Him. The fleshly senses, the mighty intellect, the supernaturally endowed soul, all were free. Man walked in the Paradise of Eden its lord and master, in the glorious liberty of the son of GOD, and by none could he be disinherited save by his own act and deed.

But the devil, the fallen cherub, *Man's Fall.* looked on this fair work of GOD with envious hatred. He entered the Eden, whence it may be he had aforetime been banished, and under the form of a Serpent, he tried to pull man Ezek. 28. 13.

down to his own level. Attacking him subtilly through his earthly affections, through the allurements of the senses, and through the pride of intellect, he offered him, through Eve, the bait of sin ; and Man, the creature of a day, presumed to question the Truth of GOD, his Almighty Creator, and then he fell. He had stooped of his own unconstrained will to listen to the serpent, and thus gave the devil the advantage over him, and man received a deadly wound ; the poison of sin passed forthwith into his blood, and the fair Image of GOD was thereby blurred and defaced ; the supernatural powers of the soul were blunted ; the clear vision of GOD was darkened, thenceforth he saw Him but as through a glass darkly ; the keen sense of conscience was perturbed ; the judgment was warped ; the Flesh became subject to death ; Faith grew dark ; Hope was almost crushed by the vivid consciousness of guilt ; Love was well nigh lost in fear ; Free-will alone remained unviolated. Satan could not, cannot touch this ; it is the Breath of GOD, and it has survived to maintain the deadly struggle which then sprang up and still exists between the flesh and the spirit.

Man had fallen, but not irretrievably ; not as Satan and his angels had fallen. He had taken the poison of death, but GOD had prepared an antidote, and His unchanging purposes of mercy changed not. Man was cast out of Eden, but he bore thence the promise of life, and grace, and restoration.

In the Eternal Counsels of the Godhead man had been created in the Likeness of GOD. The Eternal Counsels of GOD stood. " Let GOD be true, but every man a liar." Man had been made for GOD, and he could not contravene the Decree of the Most High. He might deface, but he could not efface, the Divine Image and Likeness. Human nature, that it might be restored, (and that thus the Eternal Counsel might stand,) was taken into the Divine, and thus rendered eternally glorious, GOD set His seal upon it for ever in the Incarnation. S. Jo. 1. 12-14.

THE INCARNATION.

The Prayer.

O Blessed GOD, when Thou didst will to make known the mystery of Thy Incarnation to the pure and spotless Virgin, Thou didst choose the lips of the highest Archangel for Thy message. What am I that my unclean lips should dare to speak of this so great, so aweful Mystery? And in very truth, LORD, except Thou hadst Thyself in the unfathomable depth of Thy profound, incomprehensible Humility, except Thou hadst Thyself vouchsafed in Thy all-holy Sacrament to come and dwell within this body and soul of mine, I think I had not dared even to meditate upon this tremendous Mystery, before which my whole being prostrates itself in lowliest adoration. O my GOD, enter not into judgment with Thy Servant. Forgive me however I may have heretofore sinned in any presumption in speaking or thinking of this transcendent Mystery. Now, at least, bear with me while I venture to meditate upon Thee, and guide me aright that I sin not.

V. THE INCARNATION.

The Texts.

a Ge. 3. 23, 24.
b Ro. 6. 19-21.
c Rom. 8. 5-8.
d Mal. 3. 9.
e Mal. 1. 6.
f 1 Cor. 6. 15.
g 1 Cor. 6. 19, 20.
h Gal. 5. 19-21.

1. Man fell, and by his fall separated himself from GOD, and consequently from holiness; that is, from that grace, or gift which coming from the Creator makes the creature holy: not only by separating himself from GOD did he wrong himself, but he also wronged his Creator by robbing Him of the service due to Him from His creature, by using his will, his mind, his body which were given him to be instruments of service, as weapons to make war against his LORD.

1. *Effect of the Fall.*

2. Before man could be restored he must re-unite himself to GOD, and regain the Grace he had lost, this was beyond the power of his weakened and degraded nature: he must render to GOD a service equal in value to that of which he had robbed Him, he had nothing to pay that service with, his disunion from GOD depriving him of all power to do so.

2. Man's inability to make Reparation.

a Ro. 7. 23, 24.

b Ro. 3. 9, 10.
c Ps. 14. 1-3.

3. What man could not do of himself, GOD determined to do for him, and by him, and in him: when the fulness of time was come the Eternal Word, the Second Person of the Eternal Godhead descended, and without laying aside one jot or tittle of His Divine Nature, which was impossible, united Himself wholly, and for ever, to the nature of man, and this without partaking of the sin of man, for by the power of the HOLY GHOST, the human Body which He assumed was formed for Him in the womb of an unstained Virgin.

3. God-Incarnate.

a He. 2. 14-17.
b 1 Tim. 3. 16.
c 1 S. Jo. 3. 16.
d S. Jo. 1. 1, 14.
e Heb. 1. 2, 3.
f S. Jo. 14. 9.
g Heb. 10. 12.
h He. 4. 14. 15.
i S. Lu. 1. 26-35.
j S. Mat. 1. 20-25.

4. GOD and Man were now once more united, and sanctifying grace could once more flow back into the nature which had lost it: but this was not enough; man must pay to GOD the service of which he had robbed Him, for thousands of years GOD had been robbed of His due by millions of men. Who could repay so vast a debt? The Man could

4. God-Man, the Perfect Mediator.

a Ro. 5. 8-11.
b Heb. 10. 19, 20.

^c Zech. 13. 7. Who was the Fellow of the LORD of Hosts, and so for three-and-thirty years He paid a
^d Heb. 5. 5-9. service of unfaltering obedience, and became
^e 1 Tim. 2.5,6.
^f Col. 2. 9. obedient unto death, even the death of the
^g Heb. 10. 14. Cross, this satisfaction was infinite, for it was
^h Col. 1. 14-20.
the work of GOD, it would suffice for men, for it was the work of Man.

^a Acts 2. 22, 33; 5. But death could not hold GOD-   *5. Man taken up with God, in-*
^b Col. 3. 1. Man in his chains, by His own *to Heaven.*
^c Acts 1. 11. Power He broke them, rose again, and bore into Heaven the Nature He had redeemed.

The Meditation.

Man had fallen; he had sinned against an Infinite GOD: the offence inasmuch as it was against GOD, was, yea is,—an in-   *What Sin is.*
finite offence.

Sin had severed man from GOD; there was a great gulf between the creature and the Creator, deep as hell, impassable as death, wide as the distance from earth to heaven. The Dignity and Majesty of GOD had been insulted; the clay of the earth created of nothing had dared to lift up itself against the LORD of Lords, and GOD of Gods. Who was there to make Infinite Reparation? Who could re-unite man fallen so low to GOD Who sitteth in the highest Throne? Who could bridge this yawning gulf? Where was the Mediator Who could at once touch heaven and earth? Where was the Daysman Who could make due satisfaction to the offended Majesty of GOD? Behold, He chargeth His Angels with folly, and the heavens are not pure in His sight, and how shall sinful man stand before Him?

There was but one way, and the Infinite Love of GOD begat this way, and by the Cross He made of the Way, the Life, (Via, ViTa,) and both the Way and the Life were hidden in the Truth, (VerITAs.) And in GOD-Incarnate was unfolded the Mystery of that Ineffable Counsel of the Blessed Trinity of which the first Adam was but the rough type and sketch. *Christ, the God-Man, the Mediator.*

Equal to the FATHER as touching His Godhead, and inferior to the FATHER as touching His Manhood, JESUS CHRIST, our LORD, Very GOD and Very Man, conceived by GOD the HOLY GHOST, by ineffable generation, born of the Ever-Virgin Mother-Maid and Maiden-Mother, JESUS CHRIST is the sole Mediator between GOD and man. S. Jo. 10. 30. S. Jo. 14. 28. S. Jo. 1. 1,14. S. Mat. 1. 18. S. Luke 2. 7. 1 Tim. 2. 5.

O Love Transcendent, Infinite, Unutterable, Thou hast found a way to make full reparation to the FATHER, in Whose bosom of love Thou art from all eternity; Thou hast won new life for the fallen but still cherished work of His hands; Thou hast caused the inextinguishable Light of

Eternal Truth to illumine the darkness of the great abyss; Thou hast gone down into hell; Thou hast ascended up into Heaven; Thou hast forded the torrent of death and made it a way for the ransomed to pass over; Thou hast leapt over the chasm, and made Thyself its indestructible bridge. Thou hast united the severed, and made of two, one. Heaven is Thy throne and earth Thy footstool. Thou hast joined together, and none can put asunder. The mystic betrothal was from eternity; the espousals were solemnised in the fulness of time; the bridal chamber was the immaculate womb of the pure Virgin; the Manhood was taken into GOD, and GOD and Man were One.

Oh, Mystery, passing speech or utterance! Faith alone can bear to look up to this giddy height, to look down into this profound abyss; and Faith itself would reel, and faint, and fail were it not for the daily re-presentation of this very Mystery, for the daily pledge of the Incarnation in the Daily Sacrifice of the Altar. Hail, Mystic Marriage of GOD and Man, I adore Thee, Mystery of Mysteries, foreshown in Adam —reflected in the Church,—Eternal Sacrament of GOD'S ordaining, of which Marriage was the faint reflection, to be consummated in pure Virginity hereafter, when the Bride shall be presented by the SON to the FATHER, and GOD shall be All in all. _{1 Cor. 15. 28.}

Draw near, O my soul, and gaze yet closer at this Mystery, for the aweful Godhead is veiled in flesh, and thine eyes, even thine, may now look upon thy GOD. Thou hast beheld man called into perfect being, created out of nothing, placed in a Paradise of delights, endowed with every grace of soul, and mind, and body,—all creatures owning his dominion in perfect happiness, bearing the unstained likeness and image of his GOD. Thou hast also seen him fallen. Now behold thy GOD-Incarnate. If man who was to fall were placed in Eden, *The first Adam and the* where shall Sinless Man find His *Second.* abode? Let S. Ambrose answer : " When Thou tookest upon Thee to deliver man, Thou didst not abhor the Virgin's womb." O my GOD, must Thou needs bear nine months of such imprisonment to make satisfaction for my abuse of the liberty in which GOD created me? O Orient Pearl of priceless worth, must Thou bury Thyself in the unfathomed but yet dark ocean of Virginal purity? In the fountain sealed, the spring shut up? Must Thou suffer from the first moment of Thy conception?

Right meetly does Thy Church fall down and worship Thee at the moment when she salutes Thee Incarnate GOD,—GOD made Man,—for in that first moment Thou didst reach the lowest deep of Thy profound humiliation; Thy life of toil, Thy crucifixion and Thy death were but the consequences of this stupendous act; Thou didst reach the lowest deep in that moment when from Thy royal throne at midnight, all things being in quiet silence, Thou didst leap down from the height of Infinite Godhead to the depth of finite infancy; when Thou, Almighty GOD, Who wast enthroned in the Highest, didst shroud Thyself in the womb of the Blessed Mary.

Adam was created perfect man; Thou wast born a helpless Infant. Adam was blessed of GOD; Thou wast made a curse for us. Adam was made the lord of all creatures; Thou wast a worm and no man, a very scorn of men, and the outcast of the people. Adam might freely eat of every tree of the Garden of GOD, save one; tears were Thy meat day and night; when Thou wast hungry they gave Thee gall to eat; when Thou wast thirsty, they gave Thee vinegar to drink. Adam heard the Voice of the LORD GOD among the trees in the garden; on the dry and barren tree of the Cross Thou didst utter Thy loud and bitter cry: My GOD, My GOD, why hast Thou forsaken Me? The LORD GOD caused a deep sleep to fall upon Adam, and he slept; hanging upon the Cross, Thou didst bow Thy thorn-crowned head, Thou didst give up the ghost, and cause Thyself to sleep the deep sleep of death. From the opened side of Adam sleeping, was that bride taken who was bone of his bone, and flesh of his flesh; from Thy pierced side as Thou didst hang dead upon the Tree, welled forth the Fount of Blood and Water, the Sacramental Wellspring of Eternal Life whence the Catholic Church, Thy Spotless Bride, received new being, was sanctified and cleansed, and made bone of Thy Bone, and flesh of Thy Flesh. Hidden in Para- Eph. 5. 30, 32. dise the Serpent had watched the sleep of the first Adam, and secretly plotted in subtilty the ruin of Eve whom he saw builded from his side; with crest erect and unabashed he showed himself openly on Calvary, and boldly struck the Second Adam, the only One among the sons of men over Whom he could claim no dominion, and whilst he exulted over Him as He slept in death, the Spotless Eve came forth from His side, and the Devil had no power over her, neither could the gates of Hell prevail against her.

Perfect Reparation had been made; full Satisfaction given; the Sacrifice was accepted; the Atonement was complete. The great Mystery hid from endless ages was made manifest. The Mystic Marriage of the true Samson was solemnised, the betrothal celebrated in time, to be consummated in eternity. The Bride was won. The Only-Begotten SON had given the ransom; He had paid never so much dowry and price; He overcame the sharpness of death, He went down into Hades; He set free His captives, He rose again in His glorified Body, King of Kings, and LORD of Lords, and He ascended into Heaven whence He came. Henceforth He is set down at the right hand of GOD waiting until the purification of His earthly Bride be fully perfected, and she be ready to be presented to the King in Shushan the Palace, not having spot, or wrinkle, or any such thing.

This Mystery of the Incarnation ever goeth on, as the SON Himself declareth: "My FATHER worketh hitherto, and I work." The HOLY GHOST, the Third Person in the Blessed Trinity, Who proceedeth from the FATHER and the SON, carrieth on that work in her, whom CHRIST JESUS, the Only-Begotten of the FATHER, purchased with His Blood; in her, His Bride, His Dove, His Undefiled One,—The Catholic Church.

THE CATHOLIC CHURCH.

The Prayer.

O GOD our FATHER, and Sweet Pelican of Mercy, JESUS CHRIST, Who dost feed Thy children, who are Thy portion, with Thine own Blood; Who when Thou didst find us, exiled from Paradise, in the desert land, in the waste howling wilderness of this world, didst alone lead us, and madest us to suck honey out of the Rock, and oil out of the flinty Rock,—Who didst feed us with fat of kidneys of wheat, and didst give us to drink of the pure blood of the grape; Who, when a mighty famine arose in the land, didst command the widow woman of Zarephath, Thy holy Church, to sustain us; and didst bring us to her at the gate of the city, even at our very entrance into the world, as she was seeking the two sticks of Thy holy Cross, wherewith in the inner chamber of her Mysteries, she might dress the handful of meal and the little oil which yet remained to her, that she and her son might eat thereof and die; hitherto by Thy never-failing Providence, though the famine hath been, GOD knoweth, sore enough in the land, and there hath not been dew nor rain these years,—hitherto, our barrel of meal hath not wasted, neither hath our cruse of oil failed; and yet, notwithstanding, O LORD our GOD, the sons of the Widow with whom Thou sojournest are sick, and the sickness has been so sore that there is no breath in them; and now, O GOD most Merciful, LORD of the living and the dead, hear the confession of Thy servant, who calleth Her sin to remembrance, and as Thou hast taken us Her sons out of Her bosom, where we were sleeping the sleep of death, and hast carried us apart into that loft where Thou abidest, and hast laid us upon Thine own bed, the chaste hard bed of the Holy Cross, even so also hear the voice of Thine Elijah, the Blessed Paraclete, Who Himself maketh intercession for us with groanings which cannot be uttered, and turn again and quicken us; revive us, and bring us back to our own home and to our Mother's bosom, so shall we know that Thou art a Man of GOD, yea, that Thou art the GOD-Man, and that the Word of the LORD, by which Thou didst promise to be with Thy Church unto the end of the world is indeed none other than the very Truth itself.

VI. THE CATHOLIC CHURCH.

The Texts.

[a] S. Jo. 14.18.
[b] S. Jo. 15.16.
[c] 1 Cor. 12.13.

1. The work of the Incarnation was not ended when the glorified

1. The Work of the Incarnation carried on by the Church.

Body of the Son of Mary was taken up into
Heaven, it was hardly more than begun; it was
to go on on earth by means of a certain, defi-
nite, and visible system to which the sons of
men could have access.

2. This system was to be carried
on among men by means of men,
to wit, the Apostles, to whom the
GOD-Man had committed, 1. Knowledge of the way of salvation, with
authority to teach it; 2. Certain outward visible
signs which were to convey the inward and invisible graces of the Incarnation to men, in a
word, the Sacraments. These chosen men were
strengthened to perform their work efficiently by
the Third Person in the Ever-blessed Trinity,
the HOLY GHOST, Who descended to dwell not
only with, but *in* them, and all who should through
them become partakers of the Grace of Life.
Nor was this system to come to an end with the
lives of those who were originally appointed its
ministers, it was to go on "to the end of the
world," through their lawful successors.

3. The Sacraments are the extension of the Incarnation. Twofold
in their nature, spiritual and sensi-
ble, they are the dual links by which man,
spiritual and material, is united to the GOD-
Man, to the Word made Flesh; and whereby

2. The Instrumentality by which God the Holy Ghost carries on the Work of the Incarnation.

3. The Sacraments the Extension of the Incarnation.

d 2 Tim. 1. 11.
e 2 Tim. 1. 13, 14.
f 2 Tim. 2. 2.

a S. Luke 24. 45-49.
b S. Jo. 17. 18.
c 2 Cor. 10. 3, 4, 7, 8.
d 2 Cor. 2. 10.
e S. Mat. 28. 18-20.
f Acts 6. 5, 6.
g Acts 8. 16, 17.
h Acts 14. 23.
i 1 Cor. 11. 23-25.
j 1 Cor. 10. 16.
k S. Jas. 5. 14, 15.
l S. Jo. 16. 13.
m 1 Tim. 4. 14.
n 2 Tim. 1. 6, 14.
o Eph. 1. 13.

p Acts 1. 26.
q 2 Tim. 2. 1, 2.
r Titus 1. 5.

a S. Jo. 3. 5.
b S. Mat. 26. 26-28.
c Acts 8. 17, &c.

alone he is rendered supernaturally able to receive the benefits of the Incarnation, summed up in the one word, Grace.

^a Eph. 2. 18-22.
^b 2 S. Pet. 1. 3, 4.

4. They are the channels through which GOD the HOLY GHOST conveys the Incarnation to man,—by which He grafts man into the Incarnation, and makes him a partaker of the Divine Nature. *4. Sacraments the Channels of Divine Grace.*

^a Col. 2. 12, 13.

5. In Baptism, He begets to supernatural life the new-created soul. *5. Baptism.*

^a Acts 8. 17.
^b 1 Cor. 6. 11.
^c 2 Cor. 1. 21, 22.
^d Eph. 1. 13.

6. By Confirmation, He consecrates and perfects its spiritual adolescence. *6. Confirmation.*

^a 1 Cor. 6. 17, 19.
^b 1 Cor. 11. 29.
^c 2 Cor. 13. 5.
^d Eph. 5. 29, 30, 32.
^e S. Jo. 6. 51, 53, 57.
^f Heb. 10. 19-22.
^g Heb. 13. 8, 15, 16.
^h Mal. 1. 11.
ⁱ Wis. 16. 20.
^j Ps. 78. 25, 26.

7. By the Blessed Eucharist He weds man, soul and body, to the Divine Spouse, GOD-Incarnate, by the most profound of all Mysteries, and thus united, not only fills them with all grace and heavenly benediction, but also enables man by, through, and with Him to Whom he is united to offer a service of perfect worship and homage to the Creator, and thus continually to repair the robbery of the Fall. *7. The Blessed Eucharist.*

^a 2 Cor. 2. 10.
^b 2 Cor. 5. 18, 19.
^c 1 Cor. 5. 3-5.
^d Acts 19. 18-20.

8. By Penance, He heals the wounds of the soul, (for on earth it is yet vulnerable.) *8. Penance.*

^a S. Mark 16. 18.
^b S. Mat. 26. 6-8, 10, 12, 13.
^c S. Jas. 5. 14.

9. By Holy Anointing, He prepares the body for its resurrection. *9. Unction of the Sick.*

10. By Holy Orders He transmits in unbroken flow the spiritual and supernatural graces of our Redemption, from the great High Priest within the Veil to those who are to be the Ministers and Stewards, the custodians and dispensers thereof.

11. In Marriage, He hallows the flesh for the propagation of them that are to be sanctified.

12. The Side of CHRIST opened after His Death closes not. Sacramental Grace ever flows from It in one pure uninterrupted stream.

10. Holy Orders.

11. Marriage.

12. The Perpetuity of Divine Grace.

^a 1 Thes. 4. 8.
^b S. John 20. 21-23.
^c Heb. 13. 5, 7, 17.
^d 1 Tim. 4. 14.
^e Heb. 4. 14.
^f Acts 20. 28.
^g 1 Cor. 4. 1.
^h 2 Cor. 4. 7.
ⁱ 2 Cor. 10. 3, 4, 8, &c.
^a 1 Cor. 7. 17.
^b 1 Cor. 7. 7, 28.
^c Heb. 13. 4.
^d Eph. 5. 30-32.
^a 2 Cor. 3. 5-8, 11.

The Meditation.

From the side of GOD-Incarnate sleeping on the Cross, His Bride the Church was taken; He ascended in His glorified Humanity to Heaven, yet according to His most sure promise, He still abides with Her. The Third Person of the Blessed TRINITY, GOD the HOLY GHOST still overshadows the Virgin-Mother, and the children who are born of Her are called the sons of GOD. The mystery which had been hidden from the beginning of the world has been made manifest; the eternal counsels of GOD are revealed to man; the battle has been fought, the victory won; GOD-Incarnate wrestling on the Cross has reopened the way to

The Office of the Church.

the Tree of Life ; the flaming sword of the cherubim is sheathed in the heart of Mary. The GOD-Man has chosen His Mystic Bride, He has kissed Her with the kisses of His mouth, and He has withdrawn Himself, and is gone. He is gone, but He is Hers, and She is His. He feedeth among the lilies of Paradise, until the day of the Resurrection break, and the shadows flee away ; and She, risen from His bed of the Cross, still goeth about the city, in the streets, and in the broad ways, seeking Him Whom Her soul loveth. He has set forth on His journey to a far country, He has returned to prepare a place for Her, whilst the disciples also furnish the upper room, where they make ready for the Marriage Supper of the Lamb.

As of old so now as we go into the city of the world, there shall meet us a Man bearing a pitcher of water ; let us follow Him. *The Church carries on the work of the Incarnation.* Wheresoever He shall go in we shall find the guest-chamber where the Master shall eat the Passover with His disciples. We cross the threshold of life bearing upon us the inherited defilement of our first parents, the mark of bondage, and the seeds of death. As surely as we inherit the life of corruption from our earthly parents before we can exist in the world, so surely must we be born of heavenly generation before we can see the kingdom of GOD. Man twofold in his nature has, in the natural sacrament of his conception, inherited the double penalty of sin in body and in soul; therefore, it must needs be that his second birth, also twofold in its nature, should be the twofold antidote of the twofold poison. Hence in the Holy Sacrament of Baptism the outward element of water is essentially and inseparably united to the inward gift of the SPIRIT, GOD having joined both together, and no man being able to separate them.

1 Cor. 15. 50.
S. John 6. 63.
S. John 3. 3, 5, 6.

S. John 3. 5.

In Baptism the soul is buried in the grave of CHRIST, and is likewise risen with Him, united to Him inseparably, made a temple of the HOLY GHOST, Which has passed into soul and body through the Sacramental channel, and grafted it into the Body of CHRIST, that as the branch draws life from the tree, so the baptized henceforth receives life from the Heart of CHRIST, which pulsates through every particle of the living body, which is the Church. It is now no longer dead, it has received the first principle of life through its union with CHRIST, and although the principle of corruption is but crucified and not wholly dead, yet the baptized dying before he commits, or before he is capable of committing, mortal sin, is of necessity saved, since he is united to the Life itself.

The Supernatural Life.

Rom. 6. 3-5.
Col. 2. 12, 13.

1 Cor. 6. 11, 17, 19.

The mysterious trinity of soul *The growth of the Supernatural Life.* and mind and body grows, developes, ripens. The germ of Life, received in Holy Baptism, is capable of attaining its full development, its consummation, and the Being wherein it dwells has also become by reason of age capable of committing mortal sin. By the laying on of Apostolic hands the Sevenfold gifts of the HOLY SPIRIT are communicated to the soul and body already rendered capable of their reception by its first ingrafting into CHRIST. Again "He showeth unto them His Hands," those pierced Hands whence streams forth glory ineffable; those uplifted Hands wherewith He blessed His Apostles, and by Whose virtue they in turn, endued with power from on high, have ever since imparted the Sevenfold Gifts of the HOLY GHOST to the baptized.

The soul has now attained its maturity, its full stature. It is capable of receiving the fulness of grace. The temple is com- *The Supernatural Food of the Soul.* pleted; the shrine is ready, and enabled to receive its Incarnate GOD.

O my GOD, help me to speak aright of Thy dread Eucharist. I adore Thee, O my GOD, Very GOD and Very Man, as in Thine incomprehensible condescension day by day Thou art found upon our altars, and round about our tents. Mystic Food of the Faithful, Hidden

Manna which the LORD hath given us to eat, Bread of Life, Sacred Lamb slain from the foundation of the world, Wine that maketh glad the heart of man, I adore Thee, and I worship Thee, and I acknowledge Thee to be the LORD.

The Life begun in CHRIST must grow by CHRIST. The heir enters into his first possession. He is led into his mother's House, who has instructed him, and he is given to drink of the spiced wine, of the juice of the pomegranate; he sits with the King at His Table, he eats His honey-comb with the honey, he receives the mystic kiss, he has found Him Whom his soul loveth. *Cant. 8. 2.*

United to CHRIST, made bone of His Bone, and flesh of His Flesh, day by day soul and body grow and are nourished by the Body and Blood of GOD-Incarnate, and the supernatural life waxes stronger and stronger, until the glory of GOD fills the House of GOD, and although the outer world perceives not, neither can mortal eye behold, yet love has apprehended the Word and kept It, and the FATHER and the HOLY SPIRIT come into that soul, and into that body, and there do they make in silence and in secresy their awful abode.

The Christian journeys ever onward until in the strength of that meat, he appears before GOD in Zion.

Apart from the life of the individual soul, the Blessed Eucharist has even a far higher and more sublime aspect still. It is the perpetual Oblation, the re-Presentation of the One Great Sacrifice, ever rising up before the Throne of the Almighty GOD. Day by day the smoke of the incense of the merits of CHRIST ascends from the golden Altar, shielding the sin-stained earth with its sweet cloud of fragrance. It is as it were GOD'S right hand of mercy restraining His left hand of justice. O mighty Sacrifice of the Altar where now as on the Cross the same CHRIST is the Priest and the same CHRIST is the Victim. JESUS CHRIST the same yesterday, to-day, and for ever. By this Offering from GOD to GOD of GOD by GOD, (for herein GOD the SON offers Himself through GOD the HOLY GHOST to GOD the FATHER, and the Sacrifice of Love is the joint-work of the Ever-Blessed TRINITY,) perfect worship is rendered to the Supreme GOD; full satisfaction made for the sins of the whole world; acceptable homage of thanksgiving is paid; and all-prevailing prayer for the living and the dead is offered.

The Sacrifice of the Altar.

The Precious Treasures of the Church, the Holy Mysteries or Sacraments, CHRIST the Head of the Church has committed to those whom He has appointed in His household to be His stewards, His ambas-

The Stewards of Christ's Mysteries.

2 Cor. 4. 1-7.
2 Cor. 5. 26.

sadors, His servants, and by the sacrament of Orders, He gives them power to baptize, to remit and retain sins, to consecrate the Blessed Eucharist, to confirm, to confer Orders, to anoint the sick, to join in holy matrimony, and to perform all offices of the priesthood with supernatural authority. This treasure of grace is in earthen vessels, but the excellency of the power is of GOD alone ; He is Supreme ; He is the Source of all Grace, and in accordance with the analogy traceable in all His natural works, He in like manner in His spiritual works conveys supernatural gifts, by certain fixed channels which He has Himself ordained, through certain outward means, by those hands, and by those only to which He has entrusted His Treasures. Is it not lawful for Him to do what He will with His own?

S. Joh. 20. 21-23.
Acts 13. 2, 3.
1 Tim. 4. 14.
S. Matt. 18. 18-20.
1 Cor. 11. 23.
Acts 8. 14-17.
1 S. Tim. 1. 12.
Titus 1. 5.
S. Ja. 5. 14, 15.
2 Cor. 10. 3-8.
2 Cor. 2. 10.
2 Cor. 4. 6, 7.

"GOD is unsearchable, we, the finite, cannot find out the Infinite to perfection, we behold Him now in part, we see through the glass darkly, according to the measure, suited to our present capacity, in which He hath revealed Himself; and as it is with Himself, so it is with His works, 'the most part of His works are hid,' we do not know exhaustively and to perfection all that marvellous and admirable order according to which He works all things after the counsel of His own will ; neither in nature

Ecclus. 16. 21.

nor in grace hath He revealed to us all of His ways ; but both in the natural and supernatural order He hath shown to us a part of His ways ; we are able to discover by natural means a certain system of operation by which the Creator ordinarily rules His creation, this we call the law of nature ; faith enables us supernaturally to behold the sacramental system, whereby the Redeemer ordinarily works out the salvation of them that are to be saved, that is the law of grace ; sometimes indeed the Creator and Redeemer acts on the natural or supernatural world by ways and means the order of which is not known to us, by extraordinary methods, the effects of which we are wont to call miracles and prodigies ; but ordinarily we are safe in assuming that neither in the natural nor in the supernatural world will He act save and except according to those laws by which reason and faith teach us He ordinarily regulates His operations."

The power to administer Sacraments whereby Grace is conveyed into the soul being of GOD alone can never be usurped by man. No man taketh this power unto himself. From hand to hand the Gift and Power of the HOLY GHOST has been transmitted in one vast unbroken network of many ramifications, yet all reaching back, and proceeding from, CHRIST Himself, the Source of Life, yea, rather the Life Itself; and dating from that first Commission which our Great High Priest Himself received from GOD the FATHER, and the irrevocable terms of the charter are these : "All power is given unto Me in Heaven and in earth. Go ye therefore, and teach all nations, baptizing them in the Name of the FATHER, and of the SON, and of the HOLY GHOST, teaching them to observe all things whatsoever I have commanded you : and, lo, I am with you always, even unto the end of the world. Amen."

To revert once more to the Individual Soul of the Christian. So long as it abides united to CHRIST its salvation is of necessity secure. But it is still free, it is not so bound that it cannot exercise its free-will. It has the inherent power to sever itself, and it may be severed from CHRIST. It has power to lose itself; it may be also cast away. It is beset with enemies ever on the alert to attack it and to ruin it, but they are powerless in themselves to hurt it. Wilful mortal sin, that is, a deliberate choice of what the soul knows to be contrary to the will of CHRIST, can alone separate the soul of the Christian from CHRIST, but this does effectually sever it. A soul in mortal sin is dead, and, albeit it is still a Member of CHRIST'S Body,

The Remedy for the Sicknesses of the Supernatural Life.

it can no more draw life from the Heart of CHRIST than a mortified limb can receive the circulation of the natural blood. For so long a time as it continues in mortal sin, it is then separated from CHRIST; it has fallen from Grace. And it would die everlastingly except GOD had prepared for it a remedy. There is no possibility of a repetition of Baptism; the soul has received the gift of supernatural life once and for ever. Nothing then can quicken a soul thus dead but the Precious Life-giving Blood of CHRIST. That stream which flowed from the Riven Side of the Dead CHRIST, and ever flows and ever will flow so long as the world lasts, can alone cleanse and wash away the guilt of sin, and impart new Life. This Blood must be applied as CHRIST has Himself commanded; this Pardon must be obtained from those to whom He has alone given authority, viz., His Apostolic Priesthood. The soul must be purged from the poison it has taken; Death and Life cannot dwell together in the same place; the one must of necessity destroy the other. Powerless in himself, man may yet obtain the Grace of repentance from GOD; the Fire of the HOLY GHOST may be rekindled in the smouldering soul, and awakened by Contrition the soul returns through Confession to give glory to GOD; by Penance (i.e. Satisfaction,) to claim the Merits of GOD; and by Absolution to receive remission of sins from GOD, and the Precious Blood of the Lamb once more quickens the soul and re-unites it to the Source of Life. Continuance and wilful persistence in mortal sin must of logical necessity end in the eternal death of the soul, because it cuts it off from the only way of Salvation, namely : union with CHRIST, the Life.

In its passage through the world the body has contracted much defilement, unknown, even to itself, and all its senses have shared in this defilement, and are weakened and soiled. The body drawing near to its Dissolution must be prepared for its Resurrection, and the HOLY GHOST bids that the sick be anointed with oil, by the Priests of the Church, who shall pray for him, and the LORD shall raise him up, and his sins shall be forgiven him. Our blessed LORD Himself vouchsafed to receive Holy Anointing from the hands of the Magdalene, the type of Penance, before His Death as the preparation of His Sacred Body for its Burial, and He pronounced a special blessing upon that deed of Faith.

The Seal of the Resurrection.

S. Jam. 5. 14-16.
S. Mar. 16. 18.
S. Mat. 26. 6-13.

Both the body and the soul of the Faithful are holy, and both are consecrated, anointed, and sanctified through the Sacraments that both may be fitted to stand before GOD.

Holy Matrimony was the First *The First-Ordained Sa-crament.* Great Sacrament of GOD'S ordaining, typifying and foreshadowing two of the deepest mysteries of the Faith, to wit: the Union of the Divine and Human Natures in the One Person of the GOD-Man, and the Union of CHRIST with His Church. Until the Incarnation Marriage was the highest and most honourable estate; after the Incarnation it ceased not to be both holy and blessed, keeping ever before the mind the memory of those two Great Mysteries, and although the Counsels of Perfection exalt Holy Virginity above it, and that is now the most perfect state, the closest following of our Ensample, CHRIST, the First Religious, the Virgin Son of a Virgin Mother, yet all men are not able to receive this Counsel, and the Church withholds not her Benediction from such, but she solemnizes, blesses, and hallows marriage, and commands that it be held honourable by all.

The life begun on earth, half mortal, half immortal, must needs die in order that it be quickened. *The Continuance of the Supernatural Life.* Matter and spirit must be severed that each may undergo its thorough purification apart, and from the womb of the grave, the soul awaiting its re-union with the body, passes into the valley of the shadow of death, where it can sin no more, neither gain merit any more, but where the work finished in its earthly aspect undergoes that fire by which its value shall be made manifest in the Last Day.

From the Porch of the Church on Earth, we pass through the Veil of the Flesh to the Left Hand or to the Right, either into the first outer darkness, or into the fuller Light of the Transepts of that Temple wherein day by day are gathered the souls of the Departed.

THE DEPARTED.

The Prayer.

O Thou Who art the Resurrection and the Life, Who art not the GOD of the dead but of the living, for all live unto Thee; Thou Who hast gone down into the pit wherein is no water, Thou Who hast risen from the gates of the Grave, Thou Who hast the keys of Hell and of Death, and Who hast Thyself vouchsafed to lift the veil from the unseen world, suffer me not in presumption but in faith, to look for one short moment into the Valley of the Shadow of Death, where many of my own kin have already gone, and whither my own feet must surely wend, how soon, Thou Alone, O LORD, knowest.

VII. THE DEPARTED.

The Texts.

^a Eph. 2. 4, 5.
^b Col. 2. 12.
^c Rom. 5. 12.
^d Eph. 4. 30.

1. Man, by his union with Incarnate GOD, wrought for him by the HOLY GHOST at his Baptism, has been made to share in the supernatural life that is in the New Adam; the principle of natural death that he inherits from the first Adam, must indeed as the inevitable result of original sin, have its temporary triumph, but it has lost its sting, it cannot slay the quickening seed of Eternal Life, and will at last be vanquished by it.

1. Supernatural Life.

^a He. 10. 26, 27.
^b Acts 1. 25.
^c S. Lu. 16. 23.
^d Rom. 6. 7.

2. He who dies in the Grace of the Incarnation abides therein. He who dies rejecting that Grace retains only the undying principle of natural life.

2. State fixed by Death.

^a Rom. 8. 1-11.
^b Rom. 8. 13.
^c Gal. 5. 7, 8.

3. Life is the Fruit of the Incarnation; the Sacraments are the extension of the Incarnation; he who is nourished by them grows day by day nearer to the stature of the Perfect Man; natural death, since it cannot separate us from the Incarnate, does not stop this process, but transfers it to another sphere, where that which began in time will be perfected in eternity; the perfection varying in beauty and glory according to the measure thereof attained in time. He who refuses to live by the

3. Growth and Decay.

Grace of the Incarnate dies spiritually, since he separates himself from the source of supernatural life; to this one, natural death fixes for eternity the state of death he had chosen in life.

4. The threshold of Time crossed, and the soul once passed within the Temple of Eternity, it can no longer do aught either to gain eternal life, hitherto despised, nor to forfeit the grace of life, hitherto faithfully kept sacred. Yet it witnesses the strife still going on in the outer Porch.[1]

4. The Soul conscious of things of earth.

a S. Joh. 9. 4;
Rev. 22. 11.
b Heb. 12. 1.
c 1 Sam. 28. 16, 17, 19.

---

[1] The extract appended appeared in a letter to the *Church Review*, February 23, 1873, whilst this little work was passing through the press.

"It is a well-known fact, capable of demonstration, that the great Fathers of the fourth and fifth centuries held and taught that the saints and martyrs of CHRIST were well acquainted with what was being done upon earth—in other words, that they can hear us if we ask them to pray to GOD for us. To mention a few names which occur to me. This was the opinion of S. Basil, both SS. Gregory, S. Chrysostom in the East; in the West of S. Ambrose, S. Augustine, S. Jerome. They did not think that the saints of JESUS were in an inferior condition to the angels of JESUS. And they, we know, are well aware when any sinner upon earth repents, for they rejoice over him.

"S. Jerome in particular is most earnest in pressing home again and again that the saints reigning above see all things in the light of GOD, and that they know what is going on in earth because 'they follow the Lamb *whithersoever* He goeth.'

"I would only add upon my own account, that I think the entire *argument* about the cloud of witnesses in the Epistle to

5. The Soul of the Faithful De- *5. Prayers of the Faithful Departed.* parted, inseparably welded into the Incarnate by the inflowing of Supernatural Sacramental Grace, is both able to praise GOD and pray, and its praises and its prayers alike ascend by the mediation of the Sacrifice of the Altar to the Throne of GOD.

6. The efficacy of the reciprocal *6. Efficacy of Prayers of and for the Departed.* prayers of the Saints without the Veil and of those within follows. Both have access to the One Fount of Grace, the Incarnate.

7. The Soul of the Lost, irrevo- *7. Prayers of the Lost unheard.* cably cut off by its own fault from the channels of Grace, is severed from the Incarnate by Whom alone it could have access to GOD; and its wailings and its prayers alike fall back into the pitiless unechoing darkness whence they try in vain to rise.

Marginal references:
a 2 Esd. 2. 31, 42, & 38-48.
b Rev. 6. 9-11.
c Rev. 8. 3-5.

a Heb. 12. 22-24.
b 2 Esd. 2. 31.
c 2 Mac. 12. 44, 45.
d S. Luke 1. 9, 10.
e 2 Mac. 15. 13, 14.

a S. Jo. 6. 53.
b S. Lu. 16. 24, 25, 27, 31.
c Eccles. 8. 8.
d Pro. 1. 24-28.
e Job 27. 8, 9.

The Meditation.

The two-fold being, Man, passes *State of Probation.* through his mortal existence, his time of probation, on earth. He knows but in

the Hebrews clearly implies that the writer believed that the ancient worthies were interested spectators of our race and our warfare. I use the word *argument* because, of course, the expression 'cloud of witnesses,' taken by itself, is capable of another meaning.—I remain yours truly, THOMAS W. MOSSMAN."

part, he is sojourning here as in a strange country, he is dwelling in a fleshly tabernacle, he is looking for a city whose builder and Maker is GOD. He is during this period but as it were in embryo, and he receives from the Sacraments that supernatural nourishment whereby he grows towards the perfect stature of CHRIST. On earth his body in its conception and birth received the poison of Death, and thereby became liable to death. This poison it revived voluntarily whenever the soul, by consent of the will, co-operating with the body, committed actual sin. Thus war sprang up between the law of the members and the law of the mind, between the desires of the soul and the desires of the flesh, so that, until the final purification of both, a perpetual contest is waged. Rom. 7. 22, 23.

The Incarnate obtained endless life for the fleshly nature He assumed, which had become passible and mortal through sin inherited from Adam, yet He did not remove the penalty of temporal death, but He obtained the Resurrection of the Flesh.

Man sins both in soul and body. The Sacraments are provided for his cure, conveying to him the full benefits of the Incarnate, being the Antidote of the poison which has passed into his human nature, making him a partaker of the Divine Nature, and supplying Grace by virtue of which the Soul is enabled to subdue the Flesh and to make it the servant, very Member, and Receptacle of GOD Incarnate.

The Body having fulfilled its period of probation is separated from the Soul, and undergoes that corruption which is the universal condition of mortal life. Returning to the earth whence it was originally taken, it awaits its final resurrection and perfection through its re-union with the Soul.

The Soul, immaterial and incapable of corruption, is violently dislodged by the decay and falling to pieces of the Tabernacle of the Body in which GOD originally placed it, and upon which it conspired to bring ruin and death. Immortal, it is yet not impassible; separated from its spouse, the body, the help-meet for it, it is imperfect and incapable of enjoying the fulness of the bliss prepared for it in the Beatific Vision, or of enduring the uttermost torments of the fires of Hell. In all respects made like unto the Perfect Man, CHRIST JESUS, regenerate man must pass through a time of separation of soul and body, and must therein abide until body and soul be re-united and ascend together to the same place where in His Glorified Human Body the GOD-Man sitteth on the Right Hand of the FATHER. If the soul have been nourished by the Sacraments, and so grafted into GOD Who ever liveth, it must needs go on losing more and more all traces of imperfection and deficiency, and increasing in purity, in brightness, in closer resemblance to the GOD-Incarnate of Whom, when in the flesh, it was made together with it a partaker; but it can sin no more, nor can it accumulate fresh merits, its time of probation being over.

If the soul have died, cut off from GOD-Incarnate, there exist for it no means of re-union. Like a child born dead, it has passed from the womb of earth into the womb of Hell, and from thenceforth there remaineth no more sacrifice for sin, but a certain fearful looking for of judgment and fiery indignation. It awaits the re-union with the incorruptible, yet not impassible, body born again, in which it must hear the sentence of that Judge Who has power to cast both body and soul into hell, and to Whom account must be given for the deeds done in the body.

"But what Christian soul, even though regenerate, even though continuing in union with the Incarnate, built upon the One Foundation, JESUS CHRIST, can contemplate going to render this account otherwise than with godly fear? Is not our GOD of purer eyes than to behold iniquity? Is He not a consuming fire, even though still GOD the SAVIOUR? And have we not heard the Apostle declaring that the fire

Heb. 12. 29.
1Cor.3.11-15

shall try every man's work of what sort it is? Dare we presume to hope in our own case, and in the case of those who have gone before us, even though it be with the sign of faith, that every one of our works which follow us will be found so perfect as to endure that scrutinizing fire? Must we not all fear, both for ourselves and others, that we shall have to suffer the loss of some thing held too dear in this life, which though it has not separated us from the Incarnate, has hindered the perfection of our union with Him? Yet glory be to His redeeming love, when we pass through the fire He will yet be with us, the flame shall not consume, it shall only purify us, we shall be saved, even though it be so as by fire. Blessed, then, are the dead which die in the LORD, they rest from their labour, the labour of working out their salvation, for it is already secured, they rest in the full assurance of perfect salvation, in the Hand of GOD, where no torment shall touch them, and which will gently purge away their dross, and try them as gold and silver is tried, that passing through fire and water, they may at length attain a wealthy place."

Isa. 43. 2.
Rev. 14. 13.
Wis. 3. 1, 6.

But those thrice blessed souls whose probation here, and purgation hereafter is complete, the spirits of just men *made perfect* are already associated with JESUS, the Mediator of the New

Heb. 12. 1, 22-24.

Testament in the heavenly Sion, in the New Jerusalem; from that blissful mountain they are "witnesses"[1] of our conflict with the powers of evil here below; nor are they uninterested spectators; made one spirit with the GOD-Man, they, with Him, earnestly desire the salvation of His elect, and long to receive them into the everlasting habitations to which they have themselves attained; these longings and desires they express in effectual fervent prayers, which perfumed and made an offering of a sweet-smelling savour by the incense of the merits of Him by Whom, to Whom, in Whom they pray, ascend to the eternal throne, and thence descend innumerable succours, countless graces, marvellous gifts of strength to the Church militant here on earth. The Church on earth bringing her sacrifice of Corn and Wine, anointed by the Oil of the HOLY GHOST, pours forth her supplication, the Church in the Heavens hears the cry of her suffering Sister on earth, and seconds that petition with her more perfect prayers. GOD hears the Church in the Heavens, and sends the gracious answer to her petition,—Fear not, thou art My people.

Rev. 5. 8.
Rev. 8. 3, 4.
S. Jam. 5. 16.
Heb. 12. 1.

Hos. 2. 21-23.

The prayers of the lost, pleading for them-

---

[1] A "witness" is one who knows, not by hearsay, not by means of the evidence of another, but from actual knowledge, and "we are compassed about with a great cloud of witnesses." What if the crystal sea before the throne of GOD, reflects to the vision of the Church in Heaven, the emerald rainbow of the Church on earth?

F

S. Luke 16. 23-31.

selves, and for their brethren still on earth, fall back into the abyss whence they attempt in vain to rise. There is no Altar from which they can ascend, no angels near but those who have fallen, no incense by whose smoke they can ascend to the throne of GOD, for the incense is the merits of CHRIST, from which by non-participation of the Sacraments, they wilfully severed themselves at that time when alone they were capable of perfect union, namely, when they were in the flesh.

Both Good and Bad await the Final Resurrection, when both the Purified and the Degraded soul shall be inseparably re-united to the imperishable body, and receive from the risen and glorified GOD-Man, CHRIST JESUS, the reward of the works done in the body, whether they be good or whether they be evil, by the final sentence at the Judgment.

THE JUDGMENT.

The Prayer.

O LORD GOD Almighty, Thou most mighty Judge Eternal, before Whom I must stand at the Last Day to give account of every thought, of every word, or every deed, teach me of Thy boundless Infinite Love so to prepare now for that dread trial, that I may not stand then before

Thee speechless; teach me now by the light of Thy HOLY SPIRIT so to examine my own conscience, and so humbly, reverently, and devoutly to confess my sins, that when the great Accuser shall bring before Thee mine offences, I may be able to show Thy Pardon and full Acquittance granted here on earth, written in Thy Blood, sealed with Thy love, and which Thou hast promised to ratify in Heaven. Acknowledge then, also, O LORD, every thought, and word, and deed of holiness, and accept it, for such it is in truth, as Thine Own, since by Thy grace alone man is enabled to think, or speak, or act meritoriously.

And, O LORD GOD most holy, O LORD most mighty, O holy and most merciful SAVIOUR, in that irrevocable Judgment condemn me not to the bitter pains of eternal death, but accept me through Thine All-prevailing Sacrifice, which day by day, whilst in this mortal flesh, Thy love enables me to plead before Thine Altar, and in which I place my sole trust and confidence, and through which alone I receive strength to work works well pleasing unto Thee.

VIII. THE JUDGMENT.

The Texts.

1. The world was made for man, and it has become corrupt through

1. *The world purified by fire.* ⁎ Rom. 8. 29

man's fall. After the resurrection it could no longer be a fit habitation for risen man, and it must therefore needs be purified. This purification will be by fire.

2. The LORD shall descend from Heaven, and all nations shall be gathered before Him. The thoughts of every heart shall be made manifest. The book of man's own conscience shall be opened. Each soul shall be its own accuser or excuser. *2. The Advent.*

3. JESUS CHRIST is the Judge. The twelve Apostles and their faithful successors will also have a certain judicial power as assessors of the great Judge. *3. The Judge.*

4. Angels will be the witnesses, separating good from bad for judgment. The souls of others will furnish concomitant evidence. *4. The Witnesses.*

5. Every work, both good and evil, will be brought into judgment, and receive its due recompense. *5. The Scrutiny.*

The Meditation.

GOD is a just GOD. His justice is the warrant for the General Judgment. In like manner as He ascended into Heaven will He come again a second time to judge the world. The Earth, our Mother, has been polluted by man's sin, and washed once by *The Judgment.*

the Deluge,—type of holy Baptism,—it must also undergo a second purification, and that purification will be by Fire. And in like manner as in the first Judgment by water, the LORD was with the righteous when he passed through the waters, and through the rivers, so that they overflowed him not ; so in the second Judgment when he shall walk through the fire it shall not burn him, neither shall the flame kindle upon him.

The First Advent of our LORD and SAVIOUR JESUS CHRIST was in silence ; at midnight; in humiliation ; in secresy, in weakness, in mercy. Silently the Little Child of Bethlehem passed through the spotless womb of His Virgin Mother, and left the Shrine as He entered it, consecrated to the Most High GOD, shut up, sealed for ever. None beheld that ineffable Birth, as none beheld the moment of the Resurrection. The chaste eyes of Mary first and alone beheld GOD manifest in the flesh. *The First Advent.*

The Second Advent of our LORD and Judge, CHRIST JESUS, shall be with a shout, with the voice of the Archangel, and with the trump of GOD, at midnight, in an hour when we think not ; at midnight shall that great cry be made ; Behold, the Bridegroom cometh ; go ye out to meet Him. He shall come in glory, surrounded by all His holy *The Second Advent.*

Angels; in Majesty unutterable, King of Kings, and LORD of Lords; clothed in a Vesture dipped in Blood, He shall come in the wrath and fierceness of Almighty GOD. Then shall sound forth His Voice of aweful might, and all they that are in the graves shall hear that Voice, and shall come forth, and the sea shall give up the dead which are in it, and death and hell shall deliver up the dead which are in them. Every knee shall bow before Him, every eye shall see Him, every tongue shall confess Him, JESUS CHRIST the LORD. All men shall stand before Him, not then to plead for mercy, for it will be the time of justice, and the tender Mercy and most sweet love of our FATHER, which plead hourly with and for us while we are on earth, make room for the exercise of His attribute of inflexible Justice. He, Who in the days of His humiliation witnessed before the unjust judge a good confession, has come in His Majesty to judge the world with equity, and to minister true judgment unto the people, and to render to every man according to that he hath done in the body, whether it be good or whether it be evil.

The minute scrutiny, the intense strictness of that Judgment cannot be exaggerated, nay, rather, it cannot be conceived. O my soul, weigh well beforehand this aweful trial; on its issue depends thine eternal weal or thine eternal woe. Now whilst thou art in the flesh thou mayest prepare for it, but there is no knowledge nor device in the grave whither thou goest. Once parted from the body thou art powerless to earn merit or demerit ; if thou hast died unjust, unjust thou shalt be still ; if filthy, filthy still ; if righteous, righteous still. The seeds of life or death, whichsoever thou shalt have sown on and in the earth, must germinate in that intermediate state until the ripened fruit shall be gathered by the Angels to be sifted before the Throne of the All-seeing GOD. .

Now thou thinkest perchance to hide in Earth's twilight the tares under the semblance of wheat, but in that day in that clear Light of the Resurrection Morning, and in the aweful glare from the penal fires of hell, where canst thou hide thine evil deeds ? how canst thou cover thy shame ? Who will then pity thee ? Thine own conscience will accuse thee ; thy Guardian Angel will bear witness against thee ; thine own unerring memory will torture thee. Even now thou art self-condemned. Each thought and word and deed of sin and shame will be ruthlessly dragged forth before the unpitying throng of men, of Angels, and Devils ; aye, before the Unpitying Face of the Blessed GOD Whose tender Mercy thou hast rejected, Whose Unbounded Love thou hast cast away, and Whose Unerring Justice thou must now feel. O my GOD, there will be no pity there! What will it be to look into that Face and read no pity there! "If Thou, our GOD, art wroth, with whom shall we find ruth?" O my soul, earth has not much bitterer woe than to look into the face of the beloved and to meet no answering gaze of love, and yet there is often a smile of love even upon the death-cold lips of those who lie before us insensible of our presence; but what will be that speechless woe when thou lookest on the Face of the GOD of Love, and seest no pity there! These very words which now thou revolvest in thy mind, O my soul, will be produced in evidence against thee, and the rocks will not hear thy cry, they will not hide thee nor will the stones fall on thee, and shield thee from the Wrath of the Lamb; but naked, and uncovered, and incapable of death, thou must stand out alone upon that awful stage before that countless multitude. O LORD my GOD, Most Loving FATHER, of Thy tender Mercy, spare me in that Day. I ask Thee now, O LORD, now when Thou canst hear me without any infringement of Thy Strict Justice, for I plead Thine Own Merits. I ask Thee now for mercy. Thou knowest, LORD, how my whole soul and being quails, and has ever quailed since it had consciousness, before the mere thought of that terrible Judgment; what will it do in the reality? Now Thou mayest spare, now Thou mayest pardon, now Thou mayest forgive. Mercy, Good JESUS, mercy. Be merciful, for if Thou wilt be extreme to mark what is done amiss, O LORD, how can I abide it?

But this Judgment, so aweful in *The Trial.* its mere anticipation, so tremendous in its ushering in, will be calm, and deliberate, and unimpassioned, in its session. Nothing will disturb the Balance of the Sanctuary, for the LORD is a GOD of knowledge, and by Him actions are weighed. The FATHER hath committed all judgment unto the SON, He shall sit in that Day on the Throne of His Glory, His Twelve Apostles shall sit with Him on twelve thrones, as judges, thousand thousands shall minister unto Him, ten thousand times ten thousand shall stand before Him, the Judgment shall be set, the books opened; all Creation shall arise, the Angels shall separate the good from the bad, these to inherit Everlasting Life, those, shame and everlasting contempt. The glorified bodies of the wise shall shine as the brightness of the firmament, and they that have turned many to righteousness as the stars for ever and ever. The nakedness of the wicked unclothed with the wedding garment, lacking the white rai- S. John 5. 22. S. Mat. 25. 31. S. Mat. 19. 28. Dan. 7. 10.

Dan. 12. 2, 3.

S. Mat. 22. 11-13. Rev. 3. 18.

ment, tremblingly awaits the outer darkness wherein to hide itself.

<small>1 Cor. 3. 13.
S. Mat. 25. 14-30.
S. Lu. 12.2,3.
1 Cor. iv. 5.
S Mat. 10.26.
S. Mat. 12.36.
1 Sam. 2. 3.
1 Cor. 13. 3.
Isa. 11. 3, 4.</small>
Every deed shall be weighed; every gift of grace accounted for; all hidden things of darkness shall be brought to light; the counsels of all hearts shall be made manifest; every secret thing shall be declared; every idle word accounted for; the motives of all actions shall be weighed; the secret springs of every deed; for He shall not judge after the sight of His Eyes, neither reprove after the hearing of His Ears, but true and righteous are His judgments, and He will search the reins and hearts, and He <small>Rev. 2. 23.</small> will give unto every one of us according to our works.

O LORD, we do indeed believe that Thou shalt come to be our Judge, therefore we pray Thee hear the Voice of Thy Widowed Bride as day by day she pleads for us before Thine Altar, and spare Thy Servants whom Thou hast redeemed with Thy Precious Blood, so that when Thy Holy Angels see upon us that Holy Sprinkling they may not cast us away, nor bind us into bundles to burn, nor set us on Thy Left Hand with the Goats, but may place us on Thy Right Hand, and may take us into Thine Eternal Fold, and safely garner us among Thy wheat. Even so, come, LORD JESUS.

The Trial over, it remains but for the just Judge

to pronounce Sentence : which must straightway be executed, for with GOD to speak is to act, to will is to do. Upon the Judgment therefore follows the Final Decision.

THE FINAL DECISION.

The Prayer.

O GOD, Who art the Truth, and the Eternal Word, when Thou speakest who can gainsay it? when Thou givest judgment who shall disannul it? when Thou condemnest, who shall revoke Thy Sentence? Thou art not a man that Thou shouldest lie, neither the son of man that Thou shouldest repent. What Thou hast said that wilt Thou do ; what Thou hast spoken that wilt Thou make good. Grant unto me therefore, O LORD, that I not may hear Thy Voice of Justice in that Last Great Day, condemning me to everlasting punishment with the wicked, but that standing with Thy Faithful, I may hear Thy Voice of Mercy bidding me enter in with them into Life Eternal, into that kingdom prepared for them from the foundation of the world, where they shall ever be with the LORD. Of Thy Mercy grant Thou me therein, O LORD, a place beneath the feet of Thine Elect.

IX. THE FINAL DECISION.

The Texts.

^a S. Mat. 25. 46.
^b 1 Sam. 15. 29.
^c 2 Thes. 1. 6. 7-10.

1. The Sentence decreed by the Unerring Judgment of GOD is final, irrevocable, unalterable. GOD is Justice.

1. The Sentence Irreversible.

^a S. Mat. 13. 48-50.
^b Rev. 21. 27.

2. The Separation of Good and Bad is Eternal.

2. The Separation Eternal.

^a Heb. 6. 4-6.
^b Heb. 10. 26.
^c S. Mat. 25. 10.
^d S. Mark 9. 43-48.

3. The Condemned severed from the Incarnate can never be reunited, for there is no other Mediator, but CHRIST-JESUS, Whom they have wilfully rejected. Their woe is Eternal, fixed, unalterable.

3. Condemnation Eternal.

^a 1 S. Joh. 3. 2.
^b S. John 6. 51, 54, 57, 58.
^c S. Jo. 10. 28.
^d Rev. 21. 4.
^e Rev. 22. 5.
^f 1 Thes. 4. 13-18.

4. The Blessed, inseparably united to the Incarnate, have obtained the Vision of GOD, and are like Him. Their Bliss is immutable, fixed, eternal.

4. Bliss Eternal.

The Meditation.

The Great Trial ended, the separation made, the irrevocable Sentence is pronounced, and the Judgment given by Him with Whom is no variableness, neither shadow of turning.

The Final End.

The Net is drawn to the Shore of Eternity, for it is full; the Session of the Judgment is ended, and the Angels come forth to sever the wicked from among the just. The Eternal Harvest is gathered in; the sheaves are safely garnered for ever; the tares are cast into that fire which is never quenched. The Bridegroom has come, and they that were ready have passed in with Him to the Marriage Feast, and the Door is shut for ever. The LORD, the GOD of Israel hath entered in by It, therefore It shall be shut. The Shepherd hath passed through It, the Porter hath opened to Him, and His sheep have known His Voice, and have followed Him, and are safely folded; none can stray from that Fold again; no evil beast can enter in. The King of kings, and LORD of Lords, has taken possession of His Everlasting Kingdom, and they who have fought valiantly and have overcome, are clothed in fine linen, white and clean; they have followed Him, and sit with Him in His Throne, even as He also overcame, and is set down with His FATHER in His Throne.

Wisdom hath builded her house; she hath mingled her Wine; she hath also furnished her Table. The King goeth in to see the wedding guests, and those He finds there without a wedding garment are bound hand and foot, and cast out into outer darkness, where is weeping and gnashing of teeth, for there their worm dieth not, neither is the fire quenched. They are cast out from the Holy City, punished with everlasting destruction from the Presence of the LORD, and from the glory of His Power; cast out into the blackness of darkness, "into the yawning Gehenna:" the Golden Gates of the Beautiful

City closed for ever against them; the Door of Mercy shut, and the aweful words spoken, "I know you not; depart from Me, ye cursed, into Everlasting Fire, prepared for the Devil and his angels." O my LORD and Merciful GOD, send now the Angel of Thy Presence, and deliver me from the burning fiery furnace. Shut not up my soul with the sinners, nor my life with the blood-thirsty. O keep my soul and deliver me, for Thou hast redeemed me, O LORD, Thou GOD of Truth. Grant that I may behold Thy Presence in righteousness, and that I may awake up after Thy Likeness, so shall I be satisfied with It. Send out Thy Light and Thy Truth that they may lead me, and bring me unto Thy Holy Hill and to Thy Dwelling, for the Everlasting Morning dawns, and the Bride hath made her-

Ezek. 43. 2. self ready. Behold the glory of the LORD cometh from the way of the East, and His Voice is like the noise of many waters: and the earth shineth with His glory. The Temple is finished; not one living stone is wanting. The Marriage Feast is spread, the Guests are assembled. The

Mal. 3. 17, 18. King hath returned and discerned between the righteous and the wicked; between him that served GOD, and him that served Him not.

The Royal Diadem is ready, the LORD of Hosts hath made up His jewels; He hath gathered His fine gold, He hath purified His silver.

The Holy Church, His Spotless Bride is on His Right Hand in a vesture of gold wrought about with divers colours, ruddy with the generous blood of the Martyrs, white with the spotless purity of Virgins, verdant with the fruitful works of Confessors, violet with the hallowed penance of Penitents. She hath put on her royal apparel, and stands in the inner court, she hath obtained favour in His sight, He hath held out to her the Golden Sceptre. She cometh up from the wilderness leaning upon her Beloved. Sorrow and sighing have fled away, and the Ransomed of the LORD have returned, and are come to Sion with songs and everlasting joy upon their heads, and they have obtained joy and gladness, for their eyes have seen the King in His Beauty, they have looked upon the Face of GOD, and they are at rest. His Name is in their foreheads, His Eternal Love within their hearts, His Endless Joy is theirs, and they shall reign with Him for ever and ever.

The Beginning and the End are One. The First and the Last are One. *It is finished.* The Work, begun in the far Counsels of Eternity, faintly shadowed forth in Eden, begun in the Incarnation, carried on by the Church, is perfected in Heaven.

He Who is Alpha and Omega hath entered into His glory, and the faithful share the joy of their LORD, and through all Eternity the everlasting Song shall echo through the eternal courts of Heaven : Amen. Blessing, and glory, and wisdom, and thanksgiving, and honour, and power, and might, be unto our GOD for ever and ever. Amen.

Surely Thou comest quickly, Amen. Even so, Come, LORD JESU. The SPIRIT and the Bride say, Come, and the thirsting children say Come. We sleep, but our heart waketh, listening for the Voice of the Beloved, and behold even now He standeth at the Door and knocketh, and maketh answer : Behold, I come quickly : hold fast that thou hast, that no man take thy crown. Him that overcometh will I make a pillar in the temple of My GOD ; and he shall go no more out : and I will write upon him the Name of My GOD, and the Name of the City of My GOD, New Jerusalem, which cometh down out of heaven from My GOD ; and I will write upon him My New Name. So be it, LORD, therefore day by day we pray in Thine own Words,

>Our FATHER,
>Which art in heaven,
>Hallowed be Thy Name ;
>Thy Kingdom come.
>Amen.

✠

AD TE DOMINE.

APPENDIX.

TEXTS OF HOLY SCRIPTURE,

Which may be meditated on in connexion with the foregoing subjects.

I. THE BEING OF A GOD.

1. THERE IS A GOD. (Page 1.)

^a GOD is a SPIRIT.

^b Canst thou by searching find out GOD? canst thou find out the Almighty unto perfection? It is as high as heaven; what canst thou do? deeper than hell; what canst thou know? The measure thereof is longer than the earth, and broader than the sea.

^c Why askest thou after My Name, seeing it is secret?

^d To whom will ye liken Me, or shall I be equal? saith the Holy One. Hast thou not known? hast thou not heard, that the Everlasting GOD, the LORD, the Creator of the ends of the earth, fainteth not, neither is weary? there is no searching of His understanding.

^e I am Alpha and Omega, the beginning and the ending, saith the LORD, Which is, and Which was, and Which is to come, the Almighty.

2. The Existence of God known both by Nature and Faith. (Page 3.)

ᵃ He that cometh to GOD must believe that He is.

ᵇ That which may be known of GOD is manifest in (*marg.* to) them; for GOD hath showed it unto them. For the invisible things of Him from the creation of the world are clearly seen, being understood by the things that are made, even His Eternal Power and Godhead.

ᶜ Surely vain are all men by nature, who are ignorant of GOD, and could not out of the good things that are seen know Him that is: neither by considering the works did they acknowledge the workmaster; but if they were astonished at their power and virtue, let them understand by them, how much mightier He is that made them. For by the greatness and beauty of the creatures proportionably the Maker of them is seen.

ᵈ He left not Himself without a witness, in that He did good, and gave us rain from heaven, and fruitful seasons, filling our hearts with food and gladness.

3. The Unity of God. (Page 3.)

ᵃ I am the LORD, and there is none else, there is no GOD beside Me.

ᵇ GOD is a SPIRIT.

ᶜ Where wast thou when I laid the foundations of the earth? declare, if thou hast understanding. Who hath laid the measures thereof, if thou knowest? or who hath stretched the line upon it? Whereupon are the foundations thereof fastened? or who laid the corner-stone thereof?

TEXTS OF HOLY SCRIPTURE. 83

ᵈ Hear, O Israel : the LORD our GOD is one LORD.

ᵉ Your FATHER in heaven is perfect.

ᶠ Hast thou not known? hast thou not heard, that the everlasting GOD, the LORD, the Creator of the ends of the earth, fainteth not, neither is weary? there is no searching of His understanding.

ᵍ GOD is Love.

ʰ And GOD said . . . I Am That I Am.

II. THE BLESSED TRINITY.

1. THE MYSTERY OF THE BLESSED TRINITY. (Page 7.)
2. THE TRINITY. (Page 8.)

ᵃ Holy, Holy, Holy, LORD GOD Almighty, Which was, and is, and is to come.

ᵇ I am Alpha and Omega, the Beginning and the Ending, saith the LORD, Which is, and Which was, and Which is to come, the Almighty.

3. THE THREE DIVINE PERSONS. (Page 8.)

ᵃ The Name of the FATHER, and of the SON, and of the HOLY GHOST.

ᵇ The LORD hath said unto Me : Thou art My SON, this day have I begotten Thee.

ᶜ He saw the Spirit of GOD descending like a dove, and lighting upon Him : and lo, a Voice from Heaven, saying, This is My Beloved SON, in Whom I am well pleased.

^d No man hath seen GOD at any time; the Only-Begotten SON, which is in the Bosom of the FATHER, He hath declared Him.

^e The Spirit of Truth . . . shall glorify Me: for He shall receive of Mine, and shall show it unto you.

^f The Comforter, which is the HOLY GHOST Whom the FATHER will send in My Name.

^g The Spirit of Truth, Which proceedeth from the FATHER.

^h Ye are not in the flesh but in the Spirit, if so be that the Spirit of GOD dwell in you. Now if any man have not the Spirit of CHRIST he is none of His.

ⁱ GOD hath sent forth the Spirit of His SON into your hearts, crying, Abba FATHER.

^j There are Three that bear record in Heaven, the FATHER, the Word, and the HOLY GHOST: and these Three are One.

4. THE FATHER. (Page 8.)

^a JESUS said . . . I proceeded forth and came from GOD.

^b The Spirit of Truth Which proceedeth from the FATHER.

^c In the beginning was the Word, and the Word was with GOD, and the Word was GOD. The same was in the beginning with GOD.

^d Eye hath not seen, nor ear heard, neither have entered into the heart of man, the things which GOD hath prepared for them that love Him. But GOD hath revealed them unto us by His Spirit: for the Spirit searcheth all things, yea, the deep things of GOD: for what man

knoweth the things of a man, save the spirit of man which is in him? Even so the things of GOD knoweth no man, but the Spirit of GOD.

ᵉ Through Him we both have access by One Spirit unto the FATHER.

ᶠ The FATHER, the Word, and the HOLY GHOST: and these Three are One.

ᵍ Unto which of the Angels said He at any time, Thou art My SON, this day have I begotten Thee? And again, I will be to Him a FATHER and He shall be to Me a SON. Unto the SON He saith, Thy Throne, O GOD, is for ever and ever.

ʰ All men should honour the SON, even as they honour the FATHER. He that honoureth not the SON, honoureth not the FATHER Which hath sent Him.

ⁱ If ye had known Me, ye should have known My FATHER also. I proceeded forth and came from GOD.

ʲ I and My FATHER are One.

ᵏ The Comforter, the HOLY GHOST, Whom the FATHER will send in My Name.

ˡ Whom I will send unto you from the FATHER, even the Spirit of Truth, Which proceedeth from the FATHER.

ᵐ This spake He of the Spirit, Which they that believe on Him should receive: for the HOLY GHOST was not yet given; because that JESUS was not yet glorified.

5. THE SON. (Page 8.)

ᵃ In Him dwelleth all the fulness of the Godhead bodily.

ᵇ He is before all things, and by Him all things consist.

^c His Name shall be called Wonderful, Counsellor, the Mighty GOD, the Everlasting Father, the Prince of Peace.

^d He that hath seen Me hath seen the FATHER. I am in the FATHER, and the FATHER in Me.

6. THE HOLY GHOST. (Page 9.)

^a GOD hath revealed them unto us by His Spirit: for the Spirit searcheth all things, yea, the deep things of GOD. For what man knoweth the things of a man, save the spirit of man which is in him? Even so the things of GOD knoweth no man, but the Spirit of GOD.

^b We both have access by One Spirit unto the FATHER.

^c There is one body, and one Spirit.

^d GOD is love.

^e The LORD is that Spirit.

7. THE GODHEAD EQUAL. (Page 9.)

^a The Grace of the LORD JESUS CHRIST, and the Love of GOD, and the Communion of the HOLY GHOST be with you all.

^b Baptizing them in the Name of the FATHER, and of the SON, and of the HOLY GHOST.

^c Holy, Holy, Holy, LORD GOD Almighty.

8. THE OPERATIONS OF THE GODHEAD. (Page 10.)

^a Verily, verily, I say unto you, The SON can do nothing of Himself, but what He seeth the FATHER do: for what things soever He doeth, these also doeth the SON likewise.

^b For the FATHER loveth the SON, and showeth Him all things that Himself doeth.

TEXTS OF HOLY SCRIPTURE. 87

ᶜ Many good works have I showed you from My FATHER. . . . If I do not the works of My FATHER, believe Me not. . . . The FATHER is in Me, and I in Him.

ᵈ When He, the Spirit of Truth is come, He will guide you into all truth : for He shall not speak of Himself; but whatsoever He shall hear, that shall He speak.

ᵉ No man can say that JESUS is the LORD, but by the HOLY GHOST. Now there are diversities of gifts, but the same Spirit. And there are differences of administrations; but the same LORD. And there are diversities of operations; but it is the same GOD which worketh all in all.

III. THE VISIBLE CREATION.

1. CREATION THE WORK OF THE TRINITY. (Page 16.)

ᵃ In the beginning GOD created the heaven and the earth.

ᵇ And the Spirit of GOD moved upon the face of the waters. And GOD said, Let there be light : and there was light.

ᶜ In the beginning was the Word, and the Word was with GOD, and the Word was GOD. The same was in the beginning with GOD. All things were made by Him; and without Him was not any thing made that was made.

ᵈ GOD, Who created all things by JESUS CHRIST.

ᵉ Thou sendest forth Thy Spirit, they are created.

2. Man recognises the Creator in Creation. (Page 17.)

ᵃ The invisible things of Him from the creation of the world are clearly seen, being understood by the things that are made, even His eternal power and Godhead.

3. God the Creator of all things. (Page 17.)

ᵃ All things were made by Him; and without Him was not any thing made that was made.

ᵇ Of Him, and through Him, and to Him are all things.

ᶜ I am the Lord, and there is none else. I form the light, and create darkness; I make peace, and create evil. I the Lord do all these things. For thus saith the Lord that created the heavens; God Himself that formed the earth and made it; He hath established it, He created it not in vain, He formed it to be inhabited; I am the Lord, and there is none else.

4. Creation the act of the Divine Will. (Page 17.)

ᵃ By the Word of the Lord were the heavens made: and all the hosts of them by the breath of His mouth. He gathereth the waters of the sea together, as it were upon an heap; and layeth up the deep, as in a treasure-house. Let all the earth fear the Lord: stand in awe of Him, all ye that dwell in the world. For He spake, and it was done: He commanded, and it stood fast.

5. Why Diversity in Creation. (Page 18.)

ᵃ See Job chapters xxxviii. xxxix. xl.

6. GOD CREATED HEAVEN AND EARTH. (Page 18.)

^a And of the angels He saith, Who maketh His angels spirits, and His ministers a flame of fire.

^b A fiery stream issued and came forth from before Him; thousand thousands ministered unto Him, and ten thousand times ten thousand stood before Him.

^c Are they not all ministering spirits, sent forth to minister for them who shall be heirs of salvation?

^d The morning stars sang together, and all the sons of GOD shouted for joy.

^e The chariots of GOD are twenty thousand, even thousands of angels, and the LORD is among them, as in the holy place of Sinai.

^f Let no man glory in men; for all things are yours; whether Paul or Apollos, or Cephas, or the world, or life, or death, or things present, or things to come; all are yours; and ye are CHRIST'S, and CHRIST is GOD'S.

IV. MAN.

1. CONDITION OF MAN WHEN CREATED. (Page 25.)

^a So GOD created man in His own image, in the image of GOD created He him; male and female created He them, and GOD blessed them.

^b And the LORD GOD formed man of the dust of the ground, and breathed into his nostrils the breath of life; and man became a living soul.

^c The LORD created man of the earth, and turned him

into it again. He gave them few days, and a short time, and power also over the things therein. He endued them with strength by themselves, and made them according to His image.

^d Counsel, and a tongue, and eyes, ears, and a heart gave He them to understand. Withal He filled them with the knowledge of understanding, and showed them good and evil. He set His eye upon their hearts, that He might show them the greatness of His works. He gave them to glory in His marvellous acts for ever, that they might declare His works with understanding. And the elect shall praise His Holy Name. Beside this He gave them knowledge, and the law of life for an heritage. He made an everlasting covenant with them, and showed them His judgments. Their eyes saw the majesty of His glory, and their ears heard His glorious voice.

^e They heard the voice of the LORD GOD.

^f [He] put the fear of man upon all flesh, and gave him dominion over beasts and fowls.

^g Thou madest him lower than the angels, to crown him with glory and worship. Thou madest him to have dominion of the works of Thy hands, and Thou hast put all things in subjection under his feet.

2. MAN'S FREE-WILL. (Page 25.)

^a GOD Himself made man from the beginning, and left him in the hand of his counsel; if thou wilt, to keep the commandments, and to perform acceptable faithfulness. He hath set fire and water before thee: stretch forth thy hand unto whether thou wilt. Before man is life and death ; and whether him liketh shall be given him.

ᵇ And when the woman saw that the tree was good for food, and that it was pleasant to the eyes, and a tree to be desired to make one wise, she took of the fruit thereof, and did eat, and gave also unto her husband with her ; and he did eat.

ᶜ Adam was not deceived, but the woman being deceived was in the transgression.

3. MAN'S FALL. (Page 25.)

ᵃ GOD created man to be immortal, and made him to be an image of His own eternity. Nevertheless through envy of the devil came death into the world, and they that do hold of his side find it.

ᵇ Know ye not, that to whom ye yield yourselves servants to obey, his servants ye are to whom ye obey; whether of sin unto death, or of obedience unto righteousness ?

ᶜ The angels which kept not their first estate, but left their own habitation, He hath reserved in everlasting chains, under darkness, unto the Judgment of the Great Day.

ᵈ Resist the devil, and he will flee from you.

ᵉ They shall perish, but Thou remainest.

V. The Incarnation.

1. Effect of the Fall. (Page 32.)

^a Therefore the LORD GOD sent him forth from the garden of Eden, to till the ground from whence he was taken; so He drove out the man.

^b Ye have yielded your members servants to uncleanness and to iniquity unto iniquity . . . . when ye were the servants of sin, ye were free from righteousness. What fruit had ye then in those things whereof ye are now ashamed? for the end of those things is death.

^c For they that are after the flesh do mind the things of the flesh; but they that are after the Spirit, the things of the Spirit. For to be carnally minded is death; but to be spiritually minded is life and peace: because the carnal mind is enmity against GOD; for it is not subject to the law of GOD, neither indeed can be. So then they that are in the flesh cannot please GOD.

^d Ye are cursed with a curse; for ye have robbed Me, even this whole nation.

^e If . . . I be a FATHER, where is Mine honour? and if I be a Master, where is My fear? saith the LORD of Hosts.

^f Know ye not that your bodies are the members of CHRIST? shall I then take the members of CHRIST, and make them the members of a harlot? GOD forbid.

^g Ye are not your own . . . . ye are bought with a price.

^h Now the works of the flesh are manifest . . . of the which I tell you before . . . . that they which do such things shall not inherit the kingdom of GOD.

2. Man's Inability to make Reparation. (Page 33.)

ᵃ I see another law in my members, warring against the law of my mind, and bringing me into captivity to the law of sin which is in my members. O wretched man that I I am! who shall deliver me from the body of this death?

ᵇ Both Jews and Gentiles are all under sin, as it is written, There is none righteous, no, not one.

ᶜ The fool hath said in his heart, There is no GOD. They are corrupt; they have done abominable works; there is none that doeth good. The LORD looked down from heaven upon the children of men, to see if there were any that did understand, and seek GOD. They are all gone aside, they are all together become filthy; there is none that doeth good, no, not one.

3. GOD INCARNATE. (Page 33.)

ᵃ Forasmuch then as the children are partakers of flesh and blood, He also Himself likewise took part of the same, that through death He might destroy him that had the power of death, that is, the Devil; and deliver them who through fear of death were all their lifetime subject to bondage. For verily He took not on Him the nature of Angels; but He took on Him the seed of Abraham. Wherefore in all things it behoved Him to be made like unto His brethren, that He might be a merciful and faithful High Priest in things pertaining to GOD, to make reconciliation for the sins of the people.

ᵇ Without controversy, great is the mystery of godliness: GOD was manifest in the flesh, justified in the

Spirit, seen of Angels, preached unto the Gentiles, believed on in the world, received up into glory.

^c Hereby perceive we the love of GOD, because He laid down His life for us.

^d In the beginning was the Word, and the Word was with GOD, and the Word was GOD. And the Word was made Flesh, and dwelt among us, and we beheld His glory, the glory as of the Only-begotten of the FATHER, full of grace and truth.

^e GOD, hath in these last days spoken unto us by His SON . . . . the brightness of His glory, and the express Image of His Person.

^f JESUS saith, . . . he that hath seen Me hath seen the FATHER.

^g This Man, after He had offered one Sacrifice for sins for ever, sat down on the right hand of GOD.

^h Seeing then that we have a great High Priest, that is passed into the heavens, JESUS, the SON of GOD, let us hold fast our profession. For we have not an High Priest which cannot be touched with the feeling of our infirmities, but was in all points tempted like as we are, yet without sin.

ⁱ The Angel Gabriel was sent from GOD . . . to a Virgin . . . and the Angel came in unto her, and said, Hail, thou that art full of grace, the LORD is with thee; blessed art thou among women. . . . . Fear not, Mary: for thou hast found favour with GOD, and, behold thou shalt conceive in thy womb, and bring forth a Son, and shalt call His name JESUS. He shall be great, and shall be called the Son of the Highest, . . . and of His kingdom there shall be no end. Then said Mary unto the

Angel, How shall this be, seeing I know not a man? And the Angel answered and said unto her, The HOLY GHOST shall come upon thee, and the power of the Highest shall overshadow thee; therefore also that Holy Thing which shall be born of thee shall be called the SON of GOD.

ʲ The Angel of the LORD appeared unto him [Joseph] in a dream, saying, Joseph, thou son of David, fear not to take unto thee Mary thy wife; for that which is conceived in her is of the HOLY GHOST. And she shall bring forth a Son, and thou shalt call His name JESUS: for He shall save His people from their sins. Now all this was done, that it might be fulfilled which was spoken of the LORD by the Prophet, saying, Behold, a Virgin shall be with child, and shall bring forth a Son, and they shall call His name Emmanuel; which being interpreted is, GOD with us. Then Joseph being raised from sleep, did as the Angel of the LORD had bidden him, and took unto him his wife: and knew her not until she had brought forth her first-born Son: and he called His name JESUS.

4. GOD-MAN, THE PERFECT MEDIATOR. (Page 33.)

ᵃ GOD commended His love toward us, in that, while we were yet sinners, CHRIST died for us. Much more then, being now justified by His Blood we shall be saved from wrath through Him. For if, when we were enemies, we were reconciled to GOD by the death of His SON, much more, being reconciled, we shall be saved by His life. And not only so, but we also joy in GOD, through our LORD JESUS CHRIST, by Whom we have now received the atonement.

ᵇ [We have] . . . brethren, boldness to enter into the holiest by the Blood of JESUS, by a new and living way, which He hath consecrated for us, through the veil, that is to say, His flesh.

ᶜ Awake, O sword, against My Shepherd, and against the man that is My fellow, saith the LORD of Hosts.

ᵈ . . . . CHRIST glorified not Himself to be made an High Priest; but He that said unto Him, Thou art My SON, this day have I begotten Thee. As He saith also in another place, Thou art a Priest for ever after the order of Melchisedec. Who in the days of His flesh, when He had offered up prayers and supplications, with strong crying and tears, unto Him that was able to save Him from death, and was heard in that He feared, (*marg.* for His piety,) though He were a Son, yet learned He obedience by the things which He suffered, and being made perfect, He became the author of eternal salvation unto all them that obey Him.

ᵉ For there is one GOD, and one Mediator between GOD and men, the Man CHRIST JESUS, Who gave Himself a ransom for all, to be testified (*marg.* a testimony) in due time.

ᶠ In Him dwelleth all the fulness of the Godhead bodily.

ᵍ By one offering He hath perfected for ever them that are sanctified.

ʰ We have redemption through His [the Son of His Love] Blood, even the forgiveness of sins. Who is the Image of the Invisible GOD, the First-born of every creature; for by Him were all things created, that are in heaven, and that are in earth, visible and invisible, whether they be thrones, or dominions, or principalities, or powers: all things were created by Him, and for Him: and He is before all things, and by Him all things consist. And He is the head of the Body, the Church: Who is the beginning, the first-born from the dead; that in all things He might have the pre-eminence. For it pleased the FATHER that in Him should all fulness dwell: and, having made peace through the Blood of His Cross, by Him to reconcile all things unto Himself; by Him, I say, whether they be things in earth, or things in heaven.

5. MAN TAKEN UP WITH GOD INTO HEAVEN. (Page 34.)

ᵃ See Acts ii. 22—33.

ᵇ If ye then be risen with CHRIST, seek those things which are above, where CHRIST sitteth on the right hand of GOD.

ᶜ This same JESUS, Which is taken up from you into heaven, shall so come in like manner as ye have seen Him go into heaven.

VI. THE CATHOLIC CHURCH.

1. THE WORK OF THE INCARNATION CARRIED ON BY THE CHURCH. (Page 42.)

ᵃ I will not leave you comfortless; I will come to you.

ᵇ Ye have not chosen Me, but I have chosen you, and ordained you, that ye should go and bring forth fruit, and

H

that your fruit should remain : that whatsoever ye shall ask of the FATHER in My Name, He may give it you.

^c By one Spirit are we all baptized into one body, whether we be Jews or Gentiles, whether we be bond or free ; and have been all made to drink into one Spirit.

^d I am appointed a preacher, and an Apostle, and a teacher of the Gentiles.

^e Hold fast the form of sound words, which thou hast heard of me, in faith and love which is in CHRIST JESUS. That good thing which was committed unto thee, keep by the HOLY GHOST which dwelleth in us.

^f And the things which thou hast heard of me among [by] many witnesses, the same commit thou to faithful men, who shall be able to teach others also.

 2. THE INSTRUMENTALITY BY WHICH GOD THE HOLY GHOST CARRIES ON THE WORK OF THE INCARNATION. (Page 43.)

^a Then opened He their understanding, that they might understand the Scriptures, and said unto them, Thus it is written, and thus it behoved CHRIST to suffer and to rise from the dead the third day. And that repentance and remission of sins should be preached in His Name among all nations, beginning at Jerusalem, and ye are witnesses of these things. And, behold, I send the promise of My FATHER upon you ; but tarry ye in the city of Jerusalem until ye be endued with power from on high.

^b As Thou hast sent Me into the world, even so have I also sent them into the world.

^c Though we walk in the flesh, we do not war after

the flesh : (for the weapons of our warfare are not carnal, but mighty through GOD to the pulling down of strongholds.) Do ye look on things after the outward appearance? If any man trusts in himself that he is CHRIST'S, let him of himself think this again, that as he is CHRIST'S, even so are we CHRIST'S. For though I should boast somewhat more of our authority, which the LORD hath given us for edification, and not for your destruction, I should not be ashamed.

[d] To whom ye forgive anything, I forgive also; for if I forgave anything, to whom I forgave it, for your sakes forgave I it in the person of CHRIST.

[e] And JESUS came and spake unto them, saying, All power is given unto Me in heaven and earth. Go ye therefore, and teach all nations, baptizing them in the Name of the FATHER, and of the SON, and of the HOLY GHOST : teaching them to observe all things whatsoever I have commanded you ; and, lo, I am with you alway, even unto the end of the world. Amen.

[f] . . . And they chose Stephen . . . and Philip . . . whom they set before the Apostles ; and when they had prayed, they laid their hands on them.

[g] They were baptized in the Name of the LORD JESUS. Then laid they their hands on them, and they received the HOLY GHOST.

[h] And when they had ordained them elders in every church, and had prayed with fasting, they commended them to the LORD.

[i] I have received of the LORD that which also I delivered unto you, that the LORD JESUS, the same night in which He was betrayed took bread : and when He had

given thanks, He brake it, and said, Take, eat; this is My Body, which is broken for you : this do, in remembrance of Me. After the same manner also He took the Cup when He had supped, saying, This Cup is the New Testament in My Blood ; this do ye, as oft as ye drink it, in remembrance of Me.

^j The Cup of Blessing which we bless, is it not the Communion of the Blood of CHRIST? The Bread which we break, is it not the Communion of the Body of CHRIST?

^k Is any sick among you? let him call for the elders of the Church : and let them pray over him, anointing him with oil in the Name of the LORD : and the prayer of faith shall raise him up ; and if he have committed sins they shall be forgiven him.

^l When He, the Spirit of Truth, is come, He will guide you into all truth.

^m Neglect not the gift that is in thee, which was given thee by prophecy, with the laying on of the hands of the presbytery.

ⁿ I put thee in remembrance that thou stir up the gift of GOD, which is in thee by the putting on of my hands. That good thing which was committed unto thee, keep by the HOLY GHOST which dwelleth in us.

^o In Whom also, after that ye believed, ye were sealed with that HOLY SPIRIT of Promise.

^p [Matthias] was numbered with the eleven Apostles.

^q Thou therefore, my son, be strong in the grace that is in CHRIST JESUS. And the things that thou hast heard of us, among [by] many witnesses, the same commit thou to faithful men, who shall be able to teach others also.

ʳ For this cause left I thee in Crete, that thou shouldest set in order the things that are wanting, and ordain elders in every city, as I had appointed thee.

3. THE SACRAMENTS THE EXTENSION OF THE INCARNATION. (Page 43.)

ᵃ JESUS answered and said, . . . Verily, verily, I say, . . . Except a man be born again, he cannot see the kingdom of GOD.

ᵇ ᶜ Etcetera. See (2) above.

4. SACRAMENTS THE CHANNELS OF DIVINE GRACE. (Page 44.)

ᵃ Through Him we both have access by one Spirit unto the FATHER. Now therefore ye are no more strangers and foreigners, but fellow citizens with the Saints, and of the household of GOD; and are built upon the foundation of the Apostles and Prophets, JESUS CHRIST Himself being the Chief Corner-stone; in Whom all the building, fitly framed together, groweth unto an holy temple in the LORD: in Whom ye also are builded together for an habitation of GOD through the Spirit.

ᵇ . . . His Divine Power hath given unto us all things that pertain unto life and godliness . . . that by these ye might be partakers of the Divine Nature.

5. BAPTISM. (Page 44.)

ᵃ Buried with Him in Baptism, whereby also ye are risen with Him, through the faith of the operation of GOD, Who hath raised Him from the dead. And you, being dead in your sins and the uncircumcision of your flesh, hath He quickened together with Him, having forgiven you all trespasses.

6. Confirmation. (Page 44.)

^a Then laid they their hands on them, and they received the HOLY GHOST.

^b Ye are washed, . . . ye are sanctified, . . . ye are justified in the Name of the LORD JESUS, and by the Spirit of our GOD.

^c Now He which stablisheth us with you in CHRIST, and hath anointed us, is GOD; Who hath also sealed us, and given the earnest of the Spirit in our hearts.

^d In Whom also, after that ye believed, ye were sealed with that holy Spirit of promise.

7. The Blessed Eucharist. (Page 44.)

^a He that is joined unto the LORD is one Spirit . . . . your body is the temple of the HOLY GHOST which is in you, which ye have of GOD.

^b He that eateth and drinketh unworthily, eateth and drinketh damnation to himself, not discerning the LORD'S Body.

^c . . . Know ye not your own selves, how that JESUS CHRIST is in you, except ye be reprobates?

^d No man ever yet hated his own flesh; but nourisheth it and cherisheth it, even as the LORD the Church: for we are members of His Body, of His flesh, and of His bones. This is a great mystery: but I speak concerning CHRIST and the Church.

^e I am the Living Bread which came down from heaven: if any man eat of this Bread, he shall live for ever:

and the *Bread that I will give is My Flesh, which I will give for the life of the world. Verily, verily, I say unto you, Except ye eat the Flesh of the Son of Man, and drink His Blood, ye have no life in you. As the living FATHER hath sent Me, and I live by the FATHER: so he that eateth Me, even he shall live by Me.

f Having therefore, brethren, boldness to enter into the holiest by the Blood of JESUS, by a new and living way which He hath consecrated for us, through the veil, that is to say, His flesh; and having an High Priest over the House of GOD, let us draw near with a true heart in full assurance of faith.

g JESUS CHRIST the same yesterday, and to-day, and for ever. By Him therefore let us offer the Sacrifice of Praise to GOD continually, that is, the fruit of our lips, giving thanks to His Name. But to do good, and to communicate forget not: for with such sacrifices GOD is well pleased.

h From the rising of the sun even unto the going down of the same, My name shall be great among the Gentiles; and in every place incense shall be offered unto My Name, and a pure offering, . . . saith the LORD of Hosts.

i Thou feddest Thine own people with angels' food, and didst send them bread from heaven.

j He rained down manna also upon them for to eat, and gave them food from heaven; so man did eat angels' food.

8. PENANCE. (Page 44.)

a . . . If I forgave anything, to whom I forgave it, for your sakes forgave I it in the person of CHRIST.

b GOD, Who hath reconciled us to Himself by JESUS

CHRIST . . . hath given to us the ministry of reconciliation, to wit, that GOD was in CHRIST, reconciling the world unto Himself, not imputing their trespasses unto them; and hath committed unto us the word of reconciliation.

^c I verily . . . have judged already . . . in the Name of our LORD JESUS CHRIST, when ye are gathered together, and my spirit, with the power of our LORD JESUS CHRIST, to deliver such an one unto Satan for the destruction of the flesh, that the spirit may be saved in the day of the LORD JESUS.

^d And many that believed came, and confessed and showed their deeds. Many of them also which used curious arts brought their books together, and burned them before all men; and they counted the price of them, and found it fifty thousand pieces of silver. So mightily grew the Word of GOD and prevailed.

9. UNCTION OF THE SICK. (Page 44.)

^a They shall lay hands on the sick and they shall recover.

^b Now when JESUS was in Bethany, in the house of Simon the leper, there came unto Him a woman having an alabaster box of very precious ointment, and poured it on His head, as He sat at meat. But when His Disciples saw it, they had indignation, saying, To what purpose is this waste? . . . . When JESUS understood it, He said unto them, Why trouble ye the woman? for she hath wrought a good work upon Me. . . . For in that she hath poured this ointment on My body, she did it for My burial. Verily, I say unto you, wheresoever this gospel shall be

preached in the whole world, there shall also this, that this woman hath done, be told for a memorial of her.

^e Is any sick among you? let . . . . the elders of the Church . . . pray over him, anointing him with oil in the Name of the LORD.

10. HOLY ORDERS. (Page 45.)

^a He therefore that despiseth, [rejecteth, *marg.*] despiseth not man, but GOD, Who hath also given unto us His HOLY SPIRIT.

^b Then said JESUS to them again, Peace be unto you: as My FATHER hath sent Me, even so send I you. And when He had said this, He breathed on them, and saith unto them, Receive ye the HOLY GHOST: whose soever sins ye remit, they are remitted unto them; and whose soever sins ye retain, they are retained.

^c He hath said, I will never leave thee, nor forsake thee. Remember them which have the rule over you, . . . whose faith follow. Obey them that have the rule over you, and submit yourselves: for they watch for your souls, as they that must give account; that they may do it with joy and not with grief.

^d Neglect not the gift that is in thee, which was given thee by prophecy, with the laying on of the hands of the presbytery.

^e We have a great High Priest, that is passed into the heavens, JESUS the SON of GOD.

^f . . . The HOLY GHOST hath made you overseers to feed the Church of GOD.

^g Let a man so account of us, as of the ministers of CHRIST, and stewards of the mysteries of GOD.

ᵇ We have this treasure in earthen vessels, that the excellency of the power may be of GOD, and not of us.

ⁱ We do not war after the flesh, for the weapons of our warfare are not carnal, but mighty through GOD. . . . . Though I should boast somewhat more of our authority, . . . I should not be ashamed.

11. MARRIAGE. (Page 45.)

ᵃ As GOD hath distributed to every man, as the LORD hath called every one, so let him walk. And so ordain I in all churches.

ᵇ Every man hath his proper gift of GOD, one after this manner, another after that. If thou marry thou hast not sinned.

ᶜ Marriage is honourable in all.

ᵈ We are members of His Body, of His Flesh, and of His Bones. For this cause shall a man leave his father and mother, and shall be joined unto his wife, and they shall be one flesh. This is a great mystery.

12. THE PERPETUITY OF DIVINE GRACE. (Page 45.)

ᵃ Our sufficiency is of GOD: Who hath also made us able ministers of the New Testament . . . . If the ministration of death . . . was glorious . . . which glory was to be done away; how shall not the ministration of the Spirit be rather glorious? . . . For if that which was done away was glorious, much more that which remaineth is glorious.

VII. THE DEPARTED.

1. SUPERNATURAL LIFE. (Page 58.)

^a GOD, Who is rich in mercy, for His great love wherewith He loved us, even when we were dead in sins, hath quickened us together with CHRIST.

^b Buried with Him in Baptism, wherein also ye are risen with Him.

^c By one man sin entered into the world, and death by sin; and so death passed upon all men.

^d Grieve not the HOLY SPIRIT of GOD, whereby ye are sealed unto the day of redemption.

2. STATE FIXED BY DEATH. (Page 58.)

^a If we sin wilfully after that we have received the knowledge of the truth, there remaineth no more sacrifice for sins, but a certain fearful looking for of judgment, and fiery indignation, which shall devour the adversaries.

^b Judas by transgression fell, that he might go to his own place.

^c In hell he lifted up his eyes, being in torments.

^d He that is dead is freed from sin.

3. GROWTH AND DECAY OF THE SOUL. (Page 58.)

^a Romans viii. 1—11.

^b If ye live after the flesh, ye shall die: but if ye through the Spirit do mortify the deeds of the body, ye shall live.

^c Be not deceived; GOD is not mocked: for whatsoever a man soweth, that shall he also reap. For he that

soweth to his flesh, shall of the flesh reap corruption; but he that soweth to the Spirit, shall of the Spirit reap life everlasting.

4. THE SOUL CONSCIOUS OF THINGS OF EARTH. (Page 59.)

[a] The night cometh when no man can work. He that is unjust, let him be unjust still: and he which is filthy, let him be filthy still: and he that is righteous, let him be righteous still: and he that is holy, let him be holy still.

[b] We also are compassed about with so great a cloud of witnesses.

[c] Then said Samuel . . . The LORD hath done to him, as He spake by me: for the LORD hath rent the kingdom out of thine hand . . . and to-morrow shalt thou and thy sons be with me.

5. PRAYERS OF THE FAITHFUL DEPARTED. (Page 60.)

[a] Remember thy children that sleep. . . I, Esdras, saw upon the Mount Sion a great people, whom I could not number, and they all praised the LORD with songs.

[b] I saw under the altar the souls of them that were slain for the Word of GOD, and for the testimony which they held: and they cried with a loud voice, saying, How long, O LORD, holy and true, dost Thou not judge and avenge our blood on them that dwell on the earth? And white robes were given unto every one of them; and it was said unto them, that they should rest yet for a little

season, until their fellow servants also and their brethren, that should be killed as they were, should be fulfilled.

ᶜ Another angel came and stood at the altar, having a golden censer; and there was given unto him much incense, that he should offer it with the prayers of all saints upon the golden altar which was before the throne. And the smoke of the incense, which came with the prayers of the saints, ascended up before GOD out of the angel's hand. And the angel took the censer, and filled it with fire of the altar, and cast it into [upon] the earth.

6. EFFICACY OF PRAYERS OF AND FOR THE DEPARTED. (Page 60.)

ᵃ Ye are come unto Mount Sion, and unto the city of the living GOD, the heavenly Jerusalem, and to an innumerable company of angels, to the general assembly and Church of the first-born, which are written in heaven, and to GOD the judge of all, and to the spirits of just men made perfect, and to JESUS the Mediator of the new covenant, and to the Blood of sprinkling.

ᵇ Remember thy children that sleep, for I shall bring them out of the sides of the earth, and show mercy unto them: for I am merciful, saith the LORD Almighty.

ᶜ For if he had not hoped that they that were slain should have risen again, it had been superfluous and vain to pray for the dead. And also in that he perceived that there was great favour laid up for those that died godly, it was an holy and good thought. Whereupon he [Judas Maccabeus] made a reconciliation for the dead, that they might be delivered from sin.

ᵈ According to the priest's office, his lot was to burn

incense when he went into the temple of the LORD. And the whole multitude of the people were praying without, at the time of incense.

ᵉ There appeared a man with grey hairs, and exceeding glorious, who was of a wonderful and excellent majesty. Then Onias answered, saying, This is a lover of the brethren, who prayeth much for the people, and for the holy city, to wit, Jeremias the prophet of GOD.

7. PRAYERS OF THE LOST UNHEARD. (Page 60.)

ᵃ Then JESUS said unto them, Verily, verily, I say unto you, Except ye eat the Flesh of the Son of Man, and drink His Blood, ye have no life in you.

ᵇ He cried and said, Father Abraham, have mercy on me, and send Lazarus, that he may dip the tip of his finger in water, and cool my tongue; for I am tormented in this flame. But Abraham said, Son, remember that thou in thy lifetime receivedst thy good things, and likewise Lazarus evil things: but now he is comforted, and thou art tormented. . . . Then he said, I pray thee, therefore, father, that thou wouldest send him to my father's house: for I have five brethren; that he may testify unto them, lest they also come into this place of torment. Abraham saith unto him, They have Moses and the prophets; let them hear them.

ᶜ There is no man that hath power over the spirit, to retain the spirit; neither hath he power in the day of death; and there is no discharge in that war; neither shall wickedness deliver those that are given to it.

ᵈ Because I have called, and ye refused; I have

stretched out My hand, and no man regarded ; but ye have set at nought all My counsel, and would none of My reproof; I also will laugh at your calamity ; I will mock when your fear cometh ; when your fear cometh as desolation, and your destruction cometh as a whirlwind ; when distress and anguish cometh upon you. Then shall they call upon Me, but I will not answer.

ᵉ For what is the hope of the hypocrite, though he hath gained, when GOD taketh away his soul? Will GOD hear his cry when trouble cometh upon him?

VIII. THE JUDGMENT.

1. THE WORLD PURIFIED BY FIRE. (Page 67.)

ᵃ The whole creation groaneth and travaileth in pain together until now.

ᵇ I will also gather all nations, and will bring them down into the valley of Jehoshaphat, and will plead with them there.

ᶜ This same JESUS, Which is taken up from you into heaven, shall so come in like manner as ye have seen Him go into Heaven.

ᵈ But the day of the LORD will come as a thief in the night ; in the which the heavens shall pass away with a great noise, and the elements shall melt with fervent heat ; the earth also, and the works that are therein, shall be burned up.

ᵉ For, behold, the LORD cometh forth out of His place, and will come down, and tread upon the high places of the earth. And the mountains shall be molten under Him, and the valleys shall be cleft, as wax before the fire, and as the waters that are poured down a steep place.

2. THE ADVENT. (Page 69.)

a The LORD Himself shall descend from Heaven with a shout, with the voice of the archangel, and with the trump of GOD.

b When the Son of Man shall come in His glory, and all the holy angels with Him, then shall He sit upon the throne of His glory: and before Him shall be gathered all nations.

c And the earth shall restore those that are asleep in her, and so shall the dust those that dwell in silence, and the secret places shall deliver those souls that were committed unto them. And the Most High shall appear upon the seat of judgment, and misery shall pass away, and the longsuffering shall have an end: but judgment only shall remain, truth shall stand, and faith shall wax strong: and the work shall follow, and the reward shall be showed, and the good deeds shall be of force, and wicked deeds shall bear no rule.

d He hath appointed a day, in the which He will judge the world in righteousness by that Man Whom He hath ordained; whereof He hath given assurance unto all men, in that He hath raised Him from the dead.

e These . . . are a law unto themselves; which shew the work of the law written in their hearts, their conscience also bearing witness, and their thoughts the mean while accusing or else excusing one another: in the day when GOD shall judge the secrets of men by JESUS CHRIST according to my Gospel.

ᶠ Therefore judge nothing before the time, until the LORD come, Who both will bring to light the hidden things of darkness, and will make manifest the counsels of the hearts.

ᵍ And when your sins are brought forth, ye shall be ashamed before men, and your own sins shall be your accusers in that day. What will ye do? or how will ye hide your sins before GOD and His Angels?

3. THE JUDGE. (Page 68.)

ᵃ The FATHER .... hath committed all judgment unto the SON.

ᵇ And JESUS said unto them, Verily I say unto you, that ye which have followed Me, in the regeneration, when the Son of Man shall sit in the Throne of His Glory, ye shall also sit upon twelve thrones, judging the twelve tribes of Israel.

ᶜ Do ye not know that the Saints shall judge the world? and if the world be judged by you, are ye unworthy to judge the smallest matters? know ye not that we shall judge Angels?

4. THE WITNESSES. (Page 68.)

ᵃ The reapers are the Angels.

ᵇ He shall send His Angels with a great sound of a trumpet; and they shall gather together His Elect from the four winds, from one end of heaven to the other.

ᶜ There is joy in the presence of the Angels of GOD over one sinner that repenteth.

ᵈ The men of Nineveh shall rise in judgment with this generation, and shall condemn it. . . . The queen of the south shall rise up in the judgment with this generation, and shall condemn it.

ᵉ I say unto you, It shall be more tolerable for Tyre and Sidon at the Day of Judgment, than for you. And thou, Capernaum, which art exalted unto heaven, shalt be brought down to hell : for if the mighty works which have been done in thee had been done in Sodom, it would have remained until this day. But I say unto you, that it shall be more tolerable for the land of Sodom in the Day of Judgment, than for thee.

ᶠ And the King shall answer and say unto them, Verily, I say unto you, Inasmuch as ye have done it unto one of the least of these My brethren, ye have done it unto Me. . . Inasmuch as ye did it not to one of the least of these, ye did it not to Me.

5. THE SCRUTINY. (Page 68.)

ᵃ The LORD . . . will bring to light the hidden things of darkness, and will make manifest the counsels of the hearts.

ᵇ For we must all appear before the Judgment-seat of CHRIST; that every one may receive the things done in his body, according to that he hath done, whether it be good or bad.

ᶜ I say unto you, That every idle word that men shall speak, they shall give account thereof in the Day of Judgment.

ᵈ All that are in the graves shall hear His Voice, and shall come forth, they that have done good, unto the resurrection of Life; and they that have done evil, unto the resurrection of damnation.

* And behold, I come quickly; and My Reward is with Me, to give every man according as his work shall be.

IX. THE FINAL DECISION.

1. THE 'SENTENCE IRREVERSIBLE. (Page 76.)

* These shall go away into everlasting punishment: but the righteous into life eternal.

b The Strength of Israel will not lie nor repent: for He is not a man, that He should repent.

c It is a righteous thing with GOD to recompense tribulation to them that trouble you; and to you who are troubled, rest with us; when the LORD JESUS shall be revealed from heaven with His Mighty Angels, in flaming fire taking vengeance on them that know not GOD, and that obey not the Gospel of our LORD JESUS CHRIST: who shall be punished with everlasting destruction from the presence of the LORD, and from the Glory of His Power; when He shall come to be glorified in His Saints . . . in that Day.

2. THE SEPARATION ETERNAL. (Page 76.)

* They gathered the good into vessels, but cast the bad away. So shall it be at the end of the world: the Angels shall come forth, and sever the wicked from among

the just; and shall cast them into the furnace of fire; there shall be wailing and gnashing of teeth.

[b] There shall in no wise enter into [the City] any thing that defileth, neither whatsoever worketh abomination, or maketh a lie: but they which are written in the LAMB's Book of Life.

3. CONDEMNATION ETERNAL. (Page 76.)

[a] It is impossible for those who were once enlightened, and have tasted of the heavenly gift, and were made partakers of the HOLY GHOST, and have tasted the good Word of GOD, and the powers of the world to come, if they shall fall away, to renew them again unto repentance.

[b] For if we sin wilfully after that we have received the knowledge of the truth, there remaineth no more sacrifice for sins.

[c] The Bridegroom came; and they that were ready went in with Him to the marriage: and the door was shut.

[d] If thy hand offend thee, cut it off: it is better for thee to enter into life maimed, than, having two hands, to go into hell, into the fire that never shall be quenched; where their worm dieth not, and the fire is not quenched. And if thy foot offend thee, cut it off: it is better for thee to enter halt into life, than, having two feet, to be cast into hell, into the fire that never shall be quenched; where their worm dieth not, and the fire is not quenched. And if thine eye offend thee, pluck it out: it is better for thee to enter into the kingdom of GOD with one eye, than, having two eyes, to be cast into hell fire; where their worm dieth not, and the fire is not quenched.

4. BLISS ETERNAL. (Page 76.)

ᵃ Beloved, now are we the sons of GOD; and it doth not yet appear what we shall be: but we know that, when He shall appear, we shall be like Him; for we shall see Him as He is.

ᵇ I am the Living Bread Which came down from Heaven: if any man eat of this Bread he shall live for ever. . . . . Whoso eateth My Flesh and drinketh My Blood hath eternal life, and I will raise him up at the last day. As the Living FATHER hath sent Me, and I live by the FATHER: so he that eateth Me, he shall live by Me. This is that Bread which came down from heaven . . . . he that eateth of this Bread shall live for ever.

ᶜ I give unto them eternal life; and they shall never perish.

ᵈ And GOD shall wipe away all tears from their eyes; and there shall be no more death, neither sorrow, nor crying, neither shall there be any more pain: for the former things are passed away.

ᵉ And there shall be no night there: and they need no candle, neither light of the sun; for the LORD GOD giveth them light: and they shall reign for ever and ever.

ᶠ I would not have you to be ignorant, brethren, concerning them which are asleep, that ye sorrow not, even as others which have no hope. For if we believe that JESUS died and rose again, even so them also which sleep in JESUS will GOD bring with Him. For this we say unto you by the word of the LORD, that we which are alive, and remain unto the coming of the LORD, shall not prevent them which are asleep. For the LORD Himself shall descend from heaven with a shout, with the voice of the Archangel, and with the trump of GOD: and the dead in CHRIST shall rise first: then we which are alive and remain, shall be caught up together with them in the clouds, to meet the LORD in the air, and so shall we ever be with the LORD. Wherefore comfort one another with these words.

www.ingramcontent.com/pod-product-compliance
Lightning Source LLC
Chambersburg PA
CBHW020106170426
43199CB00009B/411